QUEST
52

STUDENT EDITION

QUEST

52

STUDENT EDITION

A FIFTEEN-MINUTE-A-DAY YEARLONG PURSUIT OF JESUS

MARK E. MOORE

WATERBROOK

QUEST 52 STUDENT EDITION

Published in the United States by WaterBrook, an imprint of Random House, a division of Penguin Random House LLC.

WATERBROOK® and its deer colophon are registered trademarks of Penguin Random House LLC.

Paperback ISBN 978-0-593-19374-7
Ebook ISBN 978-0-593-19375-4

Printed in the United States of America on acid-free paper

waterbrookmultnomah.com

2 4 6 8 9 7 5 3 1

First Edition

Interior book design by Virginia Norey

SPECIAL SALES Most WaterBrook books are available at special quantity discounts when purchased in bulk by corporations, organizations, and special-interest groups. Custom imprinting or excerpting can also be done to fit special needs. For information, please email specialmarketscms@penguinrandomhouse.com.

To my grandchildren, who will journey beyond me on the quest for Christ but who make my own journey toward sunset more delightful than the sunrise:

Jackson Howerton

Nya Moore

Dominic Moore

Duke Howerton

Rosalie Moore

Lennon Howerton

Bear Moore

Dean Howerton

Contents

Contents

Introduction

Jesus said, "The kingdom of heaven is like a merchant in search of fine pearls, who, on finding one pearl of great value, went and sold all that he had and bought it" (Matthew 13:45–46). Jesus *is* that pearl of great price. He's worth every effort to obtain him and every sacrifice required along the way. ***This is the quest—to chase after him, the pearl of great price.***

This is *my* quest. Even though I've taught about the life of Christ for twenty years at the college level, Jesus still surprises me. I keep seeing him in new and fresh ways. The deeper I dig, the higher I realize he is. The more I see of him, the less I think I really know him. He's always beyond my grasp, even when he walks beside me.

I'm reminded of an incident in the middle of Jesus's ministry. His closest disciples had been with him for more than a year. Now they were alone with him in a boat (Mark 4:35–41). A storm threatened to swallow them while Jesus was sound asleep in the stern. The men woke him. They needed all hands on deck, probably to help bail out the boat. They had no clue what Jesus could actually do. He stood up in the boat and rebuked the wind and waves, which obeyed. Instantly.

Just as quickly, the disciples' terror shifted from outside the boat to inside. They had been afraid of drowning in a storm; now they were afraid of standing in his presence. They huddled in the bow of the boat and asked, "Who is this man?" That's the question. ***This is the quest—to discover the authentic Jesus.*** Not the cartoon-figure Jesus or a haloed icon in stained glass. The real Jesus—the Jesus who wants to be known.

Perhaps you're not a religious person; many on the quest are not.

That's okay. Jesus is worth the pursuit regardless of our own past. After all, no other individual has had as much impact on our world as Jesus of Nazareth. He challenged us to love our enemies, thus reordering the rules for social engagement. He prioritized the outcast, renovating social justice. He introduced servant leadership, transforming politics. He demands that we examine our hearts and not just our behavior, revolutionizing ethics. He introduced God to the world as *Father,* thus changing the very nature of prayer. There's no part of our modern lives that hasn't been affected by Jesus of Nazareth—not education, science, religion, society, law, ethics, art, or entertainment. Therefore, he's worth pursuing. He's worth devoting a year to discovering what those first disciples discovered in the boat: he's beyond our expectations and beside us all the way.

Do you want to know him, the real Jesus? Do you want to absorb his influence so you can influence others? If so, *welcome to the quest.*

The Challenge of the Quest

In the beginning, God made humans in his own image (Genesis 1:27). Sadly, we've been "returning the favor" ever since, trying to make God look like us. It was obvious when ancient priests fashioned idols to reflect their highest ideals of war, sex, riches, and beauty. Their images revealed what they really worshipped. We may think we're more sophisticated, but we do virtually the same thing when we portray Jesus as supporting our cultural values, ethical standards, and social sensibilities.

It's most obvious with our paintings of Jesus. All over the world, images of Christ look like their creators' countrymen. He has darker skin in Africa, lighter hair in Europe, and distinct eyes in Asia. In one sense, that's fine. After all, Jesus came to earth in a recognizable physical form so we could relate to him. We all need to see Jesus in a way we can relate to. The problem comes when we assume that if he *looks* like we do, he must also *think* and *act* like we do.

Our portrayals of Jesus don't end with paintings; they extend to our preaching. We speak into existence a Jesus that reflects our own values. Virtually every nationality and ethnicity have created a Jesus for their own political and social agendas. We assume that he agrees with our cultures and lifestyles. This quest is too long and too difficult to carry our presuppositions with us, so let's shed them now. Can we admit our biases and set off on this quest with humility, honesty, and submission, determined to follow the path wherever it leads and whatever it costs?

The goal of this book is to help you do just that. Think of it as a field guide to your quest for Christ. All it can do is point you in the right direction. The quest is your own. No one can take this journey for you, although some may take it with you.

The Strategy of the Quest

The first four books of the New Testament—Matthew, Mark, Luke, and John—describe the events of Jesus's life. *Quest 52* will highlight fifty-two stories from these four biographies. These will include people Jesus met, miracles he performed, things he taught, and character traits he modeled. After you read about these incidents in the Bible, *Quest 52* will guide you through some thoughts and exercises to help you see Jesus authentically. Think of these fifty-two incidents as mile markers along the way.

Between each mile marker are five days of exercises. It's here that Jesus will meet you face to face.

- **Day 1:** Read the passage(s) from the Bible. *You must not short-circuit this step.* Read the biblical story before moving to the essay. Each essay focuses on one biblical concept from one gospel passage and answers one key question relevant to your life.

- **Day 2:** Look back to the wisdom of the Old Testament to learn more about this mile marker.

- **Day 3:** Look forward to the letters in the New Testament, where fellow pilgrims expressed their own take on this mile marker.

- **Day 4:** Discuss with fellow pilgrims what you're learning on this leg of the journey.

- **Day 5:** Put into practice what you're learning as you follow the path of Jesus.

This quest will likely demand more than we expect, but the pearl of great price is more valuable than we could imagine. So let's pursue Jesus relentlessly; he wants to be found. He may even join us along the journey. Let's begin.

Section I

The Person of Jesus

We begin our journey by looking to the person of Jesus. We're trying to discover where he came from and what drove him to his destiny of death. The **beginning** is all about his birth and the striking events surrounding his arrival. The essays about his **purpose** look at his primary motivations from the time he was twelve through his three-year ministry. The next several essays look at his **relationships,** particularly how he treated people: disciples, family, opponents, and outcasts.

Beginning: chapters 1–4
Purpose: chapters 5–8
Relationships: chapters 9–13

1

Is God Jesus?

Biblical Concept: Incarnation
Read: John 1:1–18

Who is God? Is he good? Is he all powerful? Is he one or many? Everyone—whether a pastor, celebrity, atheist, or philosopher—seems to have an opinion. Who has the authority to give an answer?

According to John 1, there's one—Jesus—who can definitively answer the question: "No one has ever seen God; the only God, who is at the Father's side, he has made him known" (verse 18). If Jesus is whom he claimed to be (God), if he did what the Bible says he did, then nothing could be more important than our quest for him. Whether or not we believe in Jesus, we can't deny that he has had more impact on humanity than any other person in history. Let's start with Jesus to answer the question, Who is God?

Jesus Is Creator

"In the beginning was the Word, and the Word was with God, and the Word was God" (John 1:1). If this sounds familiar, it should. It echoes Genesis 1:1: "In the beginning, God created the heavens and the earth."

John connected Jesus, the Word, with the God who created the world with a word. Paul, the apostle, said it like this: "By him all things were created, in heaven and on earth, visible and invisible. . . . And he is before all things, and in him all things hold together" (Colossians 1:16–17). The New Testament claims that the Creator, God, took on human flesh in the person of Jesus.

Is there evidence for this? Well, one could point to the predictions he fulfilled (Luke 24:44; John 5:39), his divine birth (Luke 1:30–35), his sinless life (Hebrews 4:15), or all the miracles he performed. However, the most remarkable (and historically verifiable) evidence is his resurrection from the dead (see chapter 49). It was this one event that transformed the world.

Ultimately, you need to make up your own mind about who Jesus is. However, you would be in good company if you declared him Lord. After all, *Jesus claimed* to have all authority (Matthew 28:18), even to forgive sins (Mark 2:10) and judge the world (John 5:24–30). His *friends affirmed* he was God's Son (Matthew 14:33), even God himself (John 20:28). Even Jesus's *enemies admitted* he was the Son of God (Matthew 27:54; Mark 15:39; Luke 23:39–43). Throughout the New Testament, we have very clear declarations that Jesus is God (John 1:18; 12:41; Romans 9:5; 2 Thessalonians 1:12; Titus 2:13; Hebrews 1:8; 2 Peter 1:1; 1 John 5:20). However, he's a different kind of divine being—one who is near.

Jesus Is Here

"The Word became flesh and dwelt among us" (John 1:14). This idea that God became flesh is called the Incarnation. And, of course, it sparks all kinds of questions like "How can God be in heaven and on earth at the same time?" Without being dismissive (because questions like this are interesting), can we just admit that they are beyond human ability to answer? Oddly, this is kind of comforting. The God I worship is greater than my capacity to comprehend.

How could I ever know the unknowable God if he didn't make himself known? We can't take a shuttle to heaven. So, if God wanted us to know him, doesn't it make sense that he would show up at our level? If you want to play with a child, what do you do? You get on the floor. That's similar to what God did in Jesus. He met us where we are.

Some of the best things we believe about God are because we've seen them in Jesus. Three are unique to Christianity:

1. **God is near.** Christianity is the only global religion where God is both personal and knowable. We're invited into a relationship with him. To this point, John 1:12 says, "To all who did receive him, who believed in his name, he gave the right to become children of God." This was a brand-new idea in the Bible, that through Jesus we can pray to God as Father, even calling him Abba (Romans 8:15; Galatians 4:6).

2. **God is love.** I think most people have no problem believing that God can love people who are considered good. But can you imagine a religion where God loved not only those who loved him but also the people who hated him or wanted nothing to do with him? This is exactly what Jesus does! Check out what he said: "Love your enemies and pray for those who persecute you" (Matthew 5:44). And he modeled that from the cross, saying, "Father, forgive them, for they know not what they do" (Luke 23:34). Only through Jesus do we know that "God show[ed] his love for us . . . while we were still sinners" (Romans 5:8).

3. **God suffers.** Now, there's a crazy idea! How could God suffer? Look through the Old Testament, and you'll find only two descriptions of God suffering (Isaiah 53; Zechariah 12:10). This is an offensive idea in many religions. Yet in Jesus we see a God who suffers for those he loves even while they're unlovely. Now, *that* is a God worth worshipping. This is a God we never could have imagined without the incarnation of Jesus.

Jesus Is Clear

This brings us full circle to John 1:18: "No one has ever seen God; the only God, who is at the Father's side, he has made him known." Without Jesus, no one would have painted God with these particular brushstrokes. Imagine how different our world would be without the example set by Jesus. He showed compassion to sinners, generosity to strangers, love to enemies, and honor to women and children. All these ideas are tied to the Incarnation.

This image of God as near, loving, and suffering isn't just a philosophical idea. It shows us how to be the best siblings, friends, and teammates. Jesus shows us the most important attributes of God. That's why, rather than asking, "Is Jesus God?" we should ask, "Is God Jesus?"

Key Points

- The entire New Testament claims that Jesus is God.

- The Incarnation is necessary if we're going to know God.

- The Incarnation isn't just a philosophical idea; it shows us how to be better people.

This Week

❏ **Day 1 (Eyes):** After reading the essay, answer this question: What is the most important thing you know about God because of Jesus?

❏ **Day 2 (Ears):** Where do you see Jesus in Psalm 2 and Psalm 110?

❏ **Day 3 (Heart):** Think about Romans 9:5, Titus 2:13, and Hebrews 1:8. Using these three verses, write a short prayer, telling God what you believe about Jesus.

❏ **Day 4 (Voice):** Discussion:
- What would it take to convince you that your brother or cousin is God's Son?
- Other than Jesus, what resources do we have to know God? How do we learn who God is?
- What might you believe about God if you knew nothing about Jesus?
- What do you believe about God because you have seen Jesus?

❏ **Day 5 (Hands):** Put into practice one aspect of the Incarnation: be present. Schedule an evening with your family when you'll shut off all screens (phones, computers, TVs, etc.).

2

Is Life Random?

Biblical Concept: Genealogy
Read: Matthew 1:1–17

Have you ever been bored reading the Bible? You can admit it; you won't get struck by lightning. The genealogies are the worst. So, why did God begin the New Testament with a boring description of Jesus's family tree?

Because the genealogy puts Jesus in real history. The gospel doesn't begin "Once upon a time." It's about real people with real problems, just like you and me.

Genealogies were a big deal for Jews. The book of Genesis includes genealogies telling the family stories of Adam, Noah, and Abraham. Through these genealogies, we can trace the entire story of salvation. This is an important point: when God saves the world, he does it through imperfect people. Adam and Eve introduced sin. Noah got drunk. Abraham denied being married to his wife. If God did his best work through these people, then perhaps we, too, can play a role in God's work in our world.

Genealogy in Matthew

Matthew did something both subtle and brilliant. (Pardon me while I geek out.) He broke down the genealogy of Jesus into three sections, each with fourteen names (Matthew 1:17). Have you ever stopped to count them? I did (which tells you something about my social life). The first and third sections do, in fact, have fourteen names. But the middle section has only thirteen names. Why?[1]

I thought that might have been all Matthew had to work with and he was just rounding up. Nope. Back in the Old Testament, that pesky middle section has *seventeen names* (1 Chronicles 3). What? Why would Matthew leave out four generations, then say there were fourteen? Did he miscount? Maybe, but remember, he was a tax collector, and they were really good when it came to numbers.

The solution is in *how* Matthew counted. He gave one person a double portion (counting that person twice, which is very Jewish). Who? David. *King* David. He's the symbolic firstborn in Jesus's genealogy. In fact, Matthew's whole book describes Jesus as the new King David. How could this be? King David committed adultery, murdered a man, and ultimately tried to cover his sin. Still, somehow he's found in Jesus's genealogy.

Inclusion of Women

Matthew's use of numbers is quite Jewish. His inclusion of women was *not*! Women were seen as second class in first-century Jewish culture. For a woman to be included in a genealogy, she would have had to be extraordinarily noble. But the women in this genealogy weren't noble. Tamar pretended to be a prostitute and slept with her father-in-law in order to have a child as an heir (Genesis 38:6–30). That's seriously messed up! Rahab was a pagan prostitute who hid the spies when Joshua led the invasion against Jericho (Joshua 2). Not exactly the poster child of morality. Ruth was a Moabite, the traditional enemy of Israel (Ruth 1:4). Bathsheba had an affair with King David (2 Samuel 11:3–4). Even Jesus's own mom was accused of having sex before she was married. Mary was an unmarried teenage mother living in a small town. She would have been bullied by peers. All these women knew the sting of gossip, yet they were the very ones chosen by God, placed in Matthew's genealogy, and used to grow the faith of future generations!

Lessons from the Genealogy

God uses people to accomplish his purposes. He doesn't usually intervene with miracles; he invests in relationships. He walks with each of us to develop us into difference makers. God uses our gifts and successes, but he can turn even our failures into faith. He never wastes pain. Regardless of your past, God has a plan for your life.

The people God uses are fallible. David was a moral mess; the women in this genealogy were scandalous. Tamar and Bathsheba survived the trauma of sexual sin. Rahab was probably a victim of poverty or culturally sanctioned human trafficking. As is so often the case, their sin was not just what they did but what was done to them. Ruth was a victim of the tragic death of her husband, compounded by racism. Yet God used them all, redeeming their pain to include them in his plan. He'll do the same with you. You can play a part in sacred history! Your name won't be included in Scripture, but there's a book of life being written in heaven right now. You have a verse to contribute, and it has eternity written all over it. You have a role to play, regardless of the pain you've experienced.

Jesus is God's Son. Humanly, Jesus was Mary's son. Legally, he was Joseph's son by adoption. Fundamentally, he was God's Son. "Like Father, like Son" has never been truer than in the case of Jesus. Though he stepped into human history through a very real genealogy, he came from the Father's side, from heaven to earth. The story of Jesus is both eternal and historical. He's the bridge that spans the divide between our physical realities and the eternity we sense in our souls. Through him, we rise beyond our own genealogies to a forever future with God.

Life isn't random. It may feel as if our relationships are disconnected and our choices make no difference. As if all is chance. But this "boring" genealogy betrays the truth that God has a plan. He's going to restore the beauty of Eden. And wonder of all wonders, you can be part of that plan.

Key Points

- Genealogies tell the story of God's salvation.
- Matthew's genealogy shows God's meticulous plan of salvation.
- The inclusion of these women reminds us that all are invited to play a role in God's plan to save the world.

This Week

❑ **Day 1 (Eyes):** After reading the essay, write a simple sentence describing what you wish God would write about your contribution to his story of salvation.

❑ **Day 2 (Ears):** Read the story of Rahab in Joshua 2 and 6. What are the similarities between her life and yours? Her faith and yours?

❑ **Day 3 (Heart):** What was it about Rahab that made her such a model of faith according to Hebrews 11:31 and James 2:25? Now read Galatians 4:4. When do you think God decided that Mary would be Jesus's mother?

❑ **Day 4 (Voice):** Discussion:
- Share a bit of your family history. Where did your family come from? Was there anyone famous or infamous in your extended family?
- What strengths and weaknesses did you inherit from your father and mother?
- Share the sentence you wrote in the day 1 exercise.
- What barriers might keep you from living up to that sentence? What resources or skills will you need to acquire or develop?

❑ **Day 5 (Hands):** This week, do one thing to acquire a resource or develop a skill you listed in the day 4 discussion.

3

Can God Use Me for Big Things?

Biblical Concept: Annunciation
Read: Luke 1:26–45

We want our lives to matter. This desire for significance comes from the Creator himself. He wove it into our spiritual DNA. It drives the majority of decisions we make: what teams we root for, what colleges we choose, and what relationships we build.

The difficulty, however, is that we want to be better than we actually are. This is certainly true for me. I want to make a difference, but I doubt my ability to do much that matters. That's why the story of Mary is so inspiring. She shows us the way to do big things for God.

God's Call, Not Our Character

Mary is honored throughout the world. Yet there's a huge gap between her biography and her legacy. She lived in Nazareth, a small town the locals laughed at (John 1:46). She was a peasant girl; her fiancé was a day laborer. Yet God chose her to give birth to his Son.

No wonder she was confused when the angel Gabriel greeted her: "O favored one, the Lord is with you!" (Luke 1:28). She couldn't figure out why such an important messenger had been sent to her. She wasn't just confused; she was concerned. Gabriel had to put her at ease to even have the conversation: "Do not be afraid, Mary, for you have found favor with God" (verse 30).

There's an important lesson here: *the impact of your life is determined not by your ability but by your availability.* God has a plan for you that's based on his goodness, not your greatness. Mary was willing to offer her life to God. That willingness is the only thing we need to be used by God for big things.

God's Power; Our Willingness

Gabriel made a wonderful and frightening announcement. Mary was going to have a child. That was great news. Not just any child—an extraordinary child. He would be Mary's son by birth but God's Son by vocation. That means he would sit on David's throne as the greatest king of Hebrew history. His kingdom would extend into eternity, having no boundaries in space and time.

Mary asked, "How will this be?" (verse 34). After all, virgins don't give birth. Nonetheless, the God who spoke life into existence could certainly populate a single womb with a word. As the angel Gabriel said, "The Holy Spirit will come upon you, and the power of the Most High will overshadow you; therefore the child to be born will be called holy—the Son of God" (verse 35). Just so we're clear, this wasn't sexual. No, it was the power of God coming upon Mary, creating life in her womb as he had done with his word in Genesis 1. This was creation, not cohabitation.

What made Gabriel's promise frightening is that Mary was engaged. In Jewish culture, engagement was a legally binding contract. If this teenage bride-to-be ended up pregnant, the contract would be broken. In fact, she could be killed. According to the Mosaic law, she could be stoned for adultery if she were unfaithful to her fiancé (Leviticus 20:10). Her reputation would be that of a tramp. Yet without hesitation, she replied, "Let it be to me according to your word" (Luke 1:38). Read that carefully. She was *wishing* that God's will would prevail regardless of the cost.

That's the secret of God using any of us for big things. It's not about our ability but about our willingness to submit to God's will. Would you risk your relationships to do something big for God? It may take that. Would you sacrifice your comfort to leave a legacy? It will demand that. Would you risk your reputation to make a difference for God? There's no other path into God's purpose than your submission: "Let it be to me."

God's Provision

All this was overwhelming for Mary. In the days ahead, she would wrestle with doubt and difficulties. She would face ridicule and rejection from family and friends. That's why God gave Mary two things he will *always* give you when you accept the challenge of his call: a reason to believe God and a relationship to sustain you.

Elizabeth was a relative of Mary. She was old and had never been able to have kids. Yet by the miraculous hand of God, she was pregnant with John the Baptist. At the beginning of Elizabeth's third trimester, Mary arrived at her door. She was barely pregnant. Yet the moment they met, the fetus in Elizabeth recognized Jesus in Mary's womb and leaped for joy (verse 41). Notice how specific Elizabeth was: "Why is this granted to me that the mother of my Lord should come to me?" (verse 43). That's a lot of importance put on an embryo. Truly Elizabeth spoke truth: "Blessed is she who believed that there would be a fulfillment of what was spoken to her from the Lord" (verse 45).

Mary would stay with Elizabeth for the next three months, likely until John was born. She witnessed God's faithfulness. Mary was encouraged by Elizabeth's mentoring. Those three months gave Mary the strength she needed to return home, to face her fiancé, and to endure a difficult pregnancy. Let this be a lesson to us. If God calls you to a task, he will always give you enough evidence to believe and the relationships you need.

You can do anything he calls you to if you will only say, "Let it be to me."

Key Points

- The impact of your life is determined not by your ability or your history but by God's call.

- To do great things for God, we must give up our own wills and be willing to say, "Let it be to me."

- When God calls you to a task, he will provide both a reason to believe and a relationship to sustain you.

This Week

☐ **Day 1 (Eyes):** As you read the essay, what similarities did you see between your situation and Mary's?

☐ **Day 2 (Ears):** Read Isaiah 9:1–7. What descriptions of Jesus are found in this prophecy?

☐ **Day 3 (Heart):** Think about Colossians 1:15–17, Hebrews 1:3, and Revelation 1:8. What do these verses say about Jesus *before* he came to earth?

☐ **Day 4 (Voice):** Discussion:

- Who are the heroes in your life that led you to a place where you could believe? These could be family members, mentors, or peers.
- If you were Mary, what would be your greatest concerns about accepting God's call? What are your greatest concerns about accepting God's will in your own life?
- What is God calling you to do with your life to bring him glory?
- What are the obstacles keeping you from your next step in fulfilling God's plan for your life?

☐ **Day 5 (Hands):** Write a short description (three sentences) of what you think God wants to do with your life over the next three to five years. Now list three action steps you need to take this year to move toward that goal.

4

Does God Play Favorites?

Biblical Concept: Nativity
Read: Luke 2:1–20

When I was about five, I distinctly remember listening to my older brother talk so freely with my father and thinking, *Dad loves him more.* My younger brother always seemed to have the attention and protection of my mother. I thought, *She loves him more.* Trust me when I say this question hits close to home: Does God play favorites? Even now I look at others who seem to be closer to God, who pray more easily, who are recognized more, and I wonder.

Yes, God Plays Favorites

It's hard to deny that God seems to play favorites. Even in this passage, Caesar Augustus reigned over the Roman Empire with immense power. Quirinius was governor of Syria (an unfriendly neighbor of Israel). He had wealth and fame. Joseph and Mary, on the other hand, had neither wealth nor power. There's virtually nothing fair in this story:

- Joseph was a day laborer who had to escort his pregnant fiancée seventy miles on foot back to Bethlehem, his ancestral home, to pay their taxes. Both their clothes and their accent showed their social status.

- Israel was under the brutal bullying from Rome. Though the historical records of this census have been lost, there's no doubt that Rome took taxes from peasants in places like Palestine.

- There wasn't even enough room for Mary and Joseph once they got to Bethlehem. The new parents stayed in a relative's house, downstairs with the animals (yes, that was a thing). Animals were kept in the home at night and fed from a trough (a manger) right next to the front door.

But God's Favorites Are Not Whom You Think

Of all the people who might have first witnessed the birth of God's Son, no one would have predicted shepherds. Shepherds were low class in Mediterranean culture. Their work caused them to be ritually unclean. And these particular shepherds were stuck on the night watch. They were marginalized even among their peers.

Yet it was these lowly shepherds that God chose to be the first witnesses of the Good Shepherd, born in the City of David. Don't miss the irony here. David was the shepherd-king whose royal heir, Jesus, was birthed in his hometown. The moment was marked with an angelic announcement: "Fear not, for behold, I bring you good news of great joy that will be for all the people. For unto you is born this day in the city of David a Savior, who is Christ the Lord" (Luke 2:10–11).

The birth of Jesus set in motion his victory over sin and death. It also revealed God's favorites—the lowly.

Throughout the Bible, we see this pattern: God exalts the humble and humbles the exalted (2 Samuel 22:28; Proverbs 29:23; Ezekiel 21:26; Matthew 23:12; Luke 14:11; 18:14; James 4:6, 10; 1 Peter 5:5–6). The idea is everywhere, but nowhere is this more obvious than with shepherds. While literal shepherds were marginalized, metaphorical shepherds were revered:

- David, the shepherd-king (1 Samuel 17:1–13)

- Elders of Israel (Jeremiah 23:1–4)

- Jesus (John 10:1–18; Hebrews 13:20; Psalm 23)

- Elders of the church (1 Peter 5:1–2)

There's a lesson in this for us: God measures value differently than we do. Our culture values possessions; God values generosity. Our culture values entertainment; God values sacrifice. Often people who are valued least by our world are honored most by our God (Luke 18:9–14). It's why Jesus prioritized children, honored widows, and called fishermen. You may think you're nothing, while God thinks you're really something. Perhaps you have no power, fame, or social status. You may have been bullied, neglected, or rejected. Well, congratulations—you may just be one of God's favorites!

What does this mean for you? Two things, at least. First, the way for you to determine your real value isn't through social media, what you own, or whom you hang out with. You've got to use God's value system. If you're like me, you weren't the first picked for kickball. Perhaps you have never been one of the teacher's favorites or voted the most likely to succeed. Nonetheless, if you are the first to share with the less fortunate, you're a favorite of God. If you trust him in spite of broken trust with family or friends, God may have a particular preference for you.

Second (and this is important), being a favorite of God gives you more responsibility, not more privilege. Not everyone has clean drinking water, opportunities, abilities, health, safe families, or the chance to hear the good news of the gospel. If you find that offensive (or find yourself defending God), perhaps you've missed a key characteristic of God. God isn't fair; he's gracious. God's gifts are never for the one who receives them. The gifts he has given you are meant to be given away.

If you have an ability, you should use it to bless someone else. If you have resources, you have the opportunity to show generosity. Every injustice in this world is due not to a resource problem but to a distribution problem. We are funnels of God's grace, not buckets of his blessings. If every Christ follower practiced this, there would be no starving children, no one drinking contaminated water, and no place on the planet where Jesus's name has yet to be heard.

If you're reading this, you're favored by God. You also have been given a significant challenge: Take care of the sheep. Let them know the Good Shepherd has come to live with them, die for them, and raise them to eternal life with him. You are both blessed by God and responsible to be a blessing to others.

Key Points

- It does seem that God plays favorites, since there's inequality in our world.

- God's favorites are the lowly, not the high and mighty.

- God favors us so we can show favor on his behalf.

This Week

❑ **Day 1 (Eyes):** How did this essay change your perspective on God's favoritism toward *you*?

❑ **Day 2 (Ears):** Read Psalm 23 and John 10:1–18. What do God and Jesus do as shepherds that you could do for others?

❑ **Day 3 (Heart):** Think about Matthew 23:12, James 4:10, and 1 Peter 5:5–6. How have you seen this principle of reversal play out in your life?

❑ **Day 4 (Voice):** Discussion:
- What kinds of injustice in this world bother you the most?
- Have you ever been anyone's favorite (a parent, coach, teacher, employer)? How did that feel?
- Do you see yourself as favored by God? In what way?
- What gifts has God given you? What grace has he shown you? How will you use those to share God's love this week?

❑ **Day 5 (Hands):** Whom do you need to share the good news of Jesus with? If you have seen him, you share him. Invite someone to coffee and share what you know, or invite someone to church so she can hear what you hear.

5

Did Jesus Know He Was God When He Was a Boy?

Biblical Concept: Jesus's Maturity
Read: Luke 2:41–52

Do you ever wonder what Jesus was like in the awkward teenage years? Did his voice ever crack while he was reading Scripture in the synagogue? Did he begin to notice pretty girls? Did he eat like a teenage boy? Did he ever sleep until noon? If you're curious what Jesus was like as a kid, you're not alone. But Scripture barely touches on Jesus's growing-up years. In fact, we have only one story of a single incident.

Why Tell *This* Story?

It's recorded in the gospel of Luke (2:41–52). Luke is the only non-Jewish writer of the entire Bible. Why would he be the only one to record a story of Jesus at age twelve? Well, because he was Greek. In his culture, biographies demanded tales about their heroes becoming men. This was true of Alexander the Great, Cyrus the Liberator, and Julius Caesar. Boyhood tales predicted what kind of men they would become. These stories were written with a specific question in mind: *Was the boy like the man?*

Luke, writing to a Greco-Roman audience, met their expectation.

Jesus the boy was, in fact, like the man. Verses 40 and 52 emphasize this point: "The child grew and became strong, filled with wisdom. And the favor of God was upon him" (verse 40). "Jesus increased in wisdom and in stature and in favor with God and man" (verse 52).

In addition, the story predicts what Jesus would ultimately accomplish. It was in *Jerusalem* at *Passover* when the sacrificial lamb was slain. Jerusalem featured the *temple,* a metaphor for Jesus's own body, where people came to meet God. He was missing for *three days,* an allusion to his resurrection. All these details paint a picture of Jesus's ultimate act of redemption.

The Jewish Background

Passover was an annual Jewish pilgrimage. It was a seven-day celebration. However, most people would leave after the main sacrifices were completed to get back home to work. Though we can't know this for sure, it appears Jesus stuck around for the teaching during the last few days of Passover while his parents, Mary and Joseph, started the trip back to Galilee.

Who leaves their kid in a big city without noticing he's gone? It's easier than you might think. You see, when Mary and Joseph went from Nazareth to Jerusalem, Jesus was a boy. Therefore, he would have traveled with the caravan of women. Since he was twelve, however, he would have gone through the rites of manhood while in Jerusalem. So, when they returned, Mary would have expected him to travel with the men. After the first full day of travel, Mary and Joseph discovered Jesus was with neither of them. Mary was remarkable, but I can imagine her saying some unpleasant things to Joseph in the heat of that moment. I can also sympathize with Joseph. In his first big parenting moment, he dropped the ball big time.

In the morning they returned to Jerusalem, hearts racing as fast as their feet. They retraced their steps, asking each stranger whether he had seen their son. Finally they found him: "After three days they found him in the temple, sitting among the teachers, listening to them and asking them questions. And all who heard him were amazed at his understanding and his answers" (Luke 2:46–47).

The Big Reveal

Mary was furious. Any mother would be. She lit into him: "Son, why have you treated us so? Behold, your father and I have been searching for you in great distress" (verse 48). I can relate, having lost my son in a public market in San Antonio. I think I know exactly what she was feeling—only my son was missing for three minutes, not three days!

Jesus was dumbfounded: "Why were you looking for me? Did you not know that I must be in my Father's house?" (verse 49). He couldn't imagine what all the commotion and fuss was about. "In my Father's house" could also be translated "about my Father's business." It's a phrase that basically means "in my Dad's stuff." Is it any surprise that "they did not understand the saying that he spoke to them" (verse 50)? Even so, Jesus continued to obey his heavenly Father by submitting to his earthly parents: "He went down with them and came to Nazareth and was submissive to them" (verse 51).

Lessons to Be Learned

The story is about Jesus. He was the same person at age twelve as he would be at age thirty. He was God's Son, devoted to God's business. Nonetheless, if you hold this story up as a mirror, it asks a question of you: Are you, at your current age, at your current spiritual stage, living your potential?

If not, there may be a reason. Jesus, fully aware that he was God's Son, submitted to the authorities God had placed over him. This may be difficult to read, but you can't be God's man or woman without submitting to the authorities he's placed over you.

If you're living under your parents' roof, they're God's authorities over you (even if they don't recognize God's authority). When you go to school, the teachers, too, are God's authorities over you. Coaches, pastors, and employers are all divine tools to shape your destiny and align you with your purpose. We're tempted to think, *But they aren't godly.* That may be true, but a person doesn't have to be godly to be an authority chosen by God. We submit to God by submitting to the authorities he's placed in our lives.

Key Points

- This story is designed to answer the question, *Was the boy like the man?*

- At age twelve, Jesus was like the adult Jesus—about his Father's business.

- Jesus was God's Son at every stage of his life. The lesson for us is to act on what we know at each stage of our spiritual journeys, to carry out the mission God has for each of us.

This Week

❑ **Day 1 (Eyes):** After reading the essay, how clearly do you know God's purpose for your life?

❑ **Day 2 (Ears):** The life of David includes a fascinating tale about submitting to God's earthly authorities. Read 1 Samuel 24. What leader do you need to show more appropriate honor to?

❑ **Day 3 (Heart):** Think about Romans 13:3–7, Ephesians 6:2–3, and 1 Timothy 5:17 and how honoring others builds our spiritual capacity.

❑ **Day 4 (Voice):** Discussion:
- What have you struggled with while going through puberty? Do you have a fun story you would be willing to share?
- What advice would you give to your younger self about the man or woman you're on your way to becoming?
- Why is submission to authority so important for spiritual growth and mental health?
- Share one area where your actions are below what your level of maturity should be at your age.

❑ **Day 5 (Hands):** "Jesus increased in wisdom and in stature and in favor with God and man" (Luke 2:52). Ask a parent, roommate, or friend to help you identify one act or discipline you have been putting off that would honor God and increase your favor with others.

6

If Jesus Was Perfect, Why Was He Baptized?

Biblical Concept: Baptism
Read: Mark 1:1–13

I remember my ninth birthday. I have no idea what gifts I opened or even whether I had a party. What made it memorable was my baptism. While I was still dripping wet, we gathered by the baptistry and circled up for prayer. I was immersed in love—the love of God and my family. As important as that moment was for me, Jesus's baptism was a much bigger deal.

The Beginning

Mark was likely the first to write a gospel and, as far as we can tell, the first to use the word *gospel* in any religious sense. *Gospel* literally means "good news," but before Mark wrote, it had been good news about the emperor or a general, such as "Our emperor has an heir" or "Our general won the war."

In the Old Testament, a similar Hebrew word refers to news about the defeat of God's enemies (2 Samuel 18:26). "Good news" thus became theological shorthand for God's deliverance, as in Isaiah 52:7:

How beautiful upon the mountains
　　are the feet of him who brings good news,
who publishes peace, who brings good news of happiness,
　　who publishes salvation,
　　who says to Zion, "Your God reigns."

Mark boosted our expectations with a couple of political titles: *Christ* (a Jewish term for "king") and *Son of God* (a common reference to the emperor). Both Roman Christians and Jewish Christians would have heard this introduction as a political challenge to the rulers of their day. Talk about setting high expectations! Jesus is the new emperor and the new king of Israel. Yet what follows forces us to change our expectations—or at least our definitions of a leader.

Baptism

Jesus started his ministry by being baptized by John the Baptist, a ragtag prophet in the desert. John dressed like a hermit and ate bugs. Why would Jesus go to him? Because John was fulfilling prophecy. He was preparing the way for the Messiah (Isaiah 40:1–3; Malachi 3:1) and turning the hearts of Israel back to their ancestral fathers (Malachi 4:5–6). Even so, shouldn't John have been baptized by Jesus rather than vice versa?

John thought so. He tried to argue with Jesus: "I need to be baptized by you, and do you come to me?" (Matthew 3:14). Jesus answered, "Let it be so now, for thus it is fitting for us to fulfill all righteousness" (verse 15). How?

Jesus was sinless, yet he was baptized for the forgiveness of sins. Some will say, "Jesus was setting an example for us." Okay, but how does setting a positive example "fulfill all righteousness"? My guess is that Jesus's baptism is a bigger deal than we've imagined. He was baptized for our sins, just as he would later be crucified for our sins. His baptism foreshadowed his own death, burial, and resurrection. It pointed forward to the Cross, just as our baptism points backward to the Cross. That's *huge*.

Three extremely rare things happened as Jesus came up out of the water. First, the heavens were torn open. Second, the *Spirit of God* descended in the visible form of a dove. Third, *God the Father* audibly spoke, saying, "You are my beloved Son; with you I am well pleased" (Mark 1:11). For the first time in human history, the entire Trinity appeared in one place; Father, Son, and Spirit met in the water when Jesus was baptized. The plan of God was unfolding in front of them. God's Son, led by the Spirit, would die for our sins and be raised again for our eternal life.

Temptation

Immediately after getting baptized, Jesus was thrust into the wilderness. Unlike Matthew and Luke, Mark didn't describe the three temptations in much detail. He shared only that Jesus was tempted for forty days.

Forty, in the Bible, tends to signal God's work among humanity. In this story, Jesus was reenacting the wilderness wandering of Israel. You might be thinking, *Wait a minute. Israel was in the desert for forty years, not forty days.* Right. But how long *should* they have been in the wilderness? Forty days!

Because of their unbelief, Israel wandered in the wilderness for forty years rather than forty days. In a sense, Jesus embodied the entire nation of Israel (as he did when he was baptized for their sins). Jesus accomplished in his wilderness temptation what the nation should have done so many years earlier.

Lessons to Be Learned

In both the baptism and the wilderness stories, Jesus stood for all Israel and reversed their mistakes. This is exactly what is offered to us when we follow him in baptism. We're immersed in Jesus, being buried as he was buried and raised as he was raised. Our mistakes are forgiven, and our lives made right. Likewise, following baptism, when we're tempted, we can lean into his life and find a way through the wilderness wandering.

Oh, we still face temptations. We still must resist. But Jesus has already defeated our Enemy and provided a model of how we can resist.

In his baptism, Jesus looked forward to his sacrifice on the cross, while in our baptism we look backward to his sacrifice and resurrection. Our very lives are incorporated into his perfect life, his sacrificial death, and his victorious resurrection. As Colossians 3:3–4 says, "You have died, and your life is hidden with Christ in God. When Christ who is your life appears, then you also will appear with him in glory." *That* is why Jesus was baptized.

Key Points

- *Gospel* literally means "good news." Originally it referred to news about earthly kings, but Jesus is the king over every kingdom.

- Jesus's baptism was for the forgiveness of sins—not his sins but our sins. This looked forward to what would happen on the cross.

- Jesus's temptation in the wilderness reversed the failure of Israel. If you walk with Jesus through your temptation, through your own past failure, he can turn your history around.

This Week

❏ **Day 1 (Eyes):** Did reading the essay change how you see baptism?

❏ **Day 2 (Ears):** Read Numbers 13–14. Where do you see yourself in the story? Are you like the ten spies who feared? Like the two who believed? Or like the crowd who refused to obey?

❏ **Day 3 (Heart):** Think about Romans 6:1–7 and 1 Corinthians 10:1–5. How do these two descriptions of baptism relate to Jesus's baptism?

❏ **Day 4 (Voice):** Discussion:

- Share a story of someone in your life who paved the way for you. It could be a sibling, parent, mentor, or coach.
- Have you ever willingly taken the blame or punishment for someone else or paid the price someone else owed? How did that feel?
- What does it mean to have your life absorbed in Jesus (Colossians 3:3–4)?
- If you haven't been baptized, what do you need to do to make that happen? What's keeping you from taking that step?

❏ **Day 5 (Hands):** Share with a close friend or mentor what you discovered about yourself in the day 2 exercise. Ask that person what she thinks you would have to do to be more committed to fully obeying God.

7

Did Jesus Have a
Life Purpose? Part I

Biblical Concept: Life Purpose
Read: Luke 19:1–10

After preaching, I often dismiss church by saying, "Let's make Jesus famous." It's not just a catchy slogan. It's a theological statement of my life purpose. To be more specific, my life purpose is to make Jesus famous by using the gifts he gave me to teach others about him. I've given a lot of thought to my life purpose. You should too. The life you want doesn't happen by accident.

Jesus stated his life purpose in John 10:10: "I came that they may have life and have it abundantly." His entire life was about giving life to others. In the Greek language, there are three words for "life." The first is *bios,* as in *biology.* It's the life we experience in the physical body and implies "physical health" (Luke 8:14). The second word is *psychē,* as in *psychology.* It speaks of our souls or minds and implies "spiritual health" or "mental health" (Matthew 16:25). But the word used in John 10:10 is *zōē,* as in *zoology.* In this context, it refers to the kind of life that comes directly from God (John 1:4). When Jesus comes into your life, his eternal life overflows from you.

How does Jesus give us this quality of life? We'll let him explain himself with his other two purpose statements. We'll begin with Luke 19:10 in this chapter, and we'll give full attention to Mark 10:45 in the next.

The Son of Man Came to Seek and Save the Lost

In the final week of Jesus's life, he made his way to Jerusalem. He took the major trade route that passed right through Jericho, the oldest continuously inhabited city on the planet. In Jesus's day, it was a well-populated and busy city, which explains why a chief tax collector like Zacchaeus made his home there.

As Jesus was passing through, expectations were flying high. Some people were ready to make him king by force. Others were prepared to force his death. His reputation for extraordinary miracles had attracted huge crowds, so some people couldn't get a front-row seat to see Jesus, including some of the rich and powerful like Zacchaeus.

Zacchaeus wasn't just a tax collector; he was in upper management of the financial system in the city. In other words, this "wee little man" was a really big deal. But as powerful as Zacchaeus was, he was also hated by those around him—and for good reason. He cheated them out of their hard-earned money and gave a cut to their Roman overlords! No wonder he was despised, which explains why he had to climb a tree to catch a glimpse of Jesus.

The crowds went wild. "Hey, Jesus, we love you!" "Hey, Jesus, hold my baby!" "Hey, Jesus, can you heal my allergies?" In the midst of the parade, Jesus suddenly stopped. He looked up into the sycamore fig tree and called Zacchaeus by name! The broad, low limbs made the tree easy to climb, and the broad, thick leaves made it easy to hide. Zacchaeus desperately wanted to see Jesus, but it's unlikely he wanted Jesus to see him. Often those up-and-comers like Zacchaeus were quite cautious with public spiritual leaders who could expose their secret lives.

Yet Jesus's invitation was irresistible: "Zacchaeus, hurry and come down, for I must stay at your house today" (Luke 19:5). The crowds were stunned. Jesus unexpectedly accepted the one everyone else rejected. But Jesus didn't just accept him; Jesus needed him. Why in the world did Jesus need Zacchaeus? As the story unfolds, we'll watch Zacchaeus preach without words to those who would never come to "church."

Zacchaeus's sudden transformation was shocking—no one saw it coming: "Behold, Lord, the half of my goods I give to the poor. And if I have defrauded anyone of anything, I restore it fourfold" (verse 8). Giving fourfold was what the law of Moses mandated (Exodus 22:1). Zacchaeus, however, started with "the law of Christ" (Galatians 6:2; James 2:8) by giving half his possessions to the poor. Jesus treated the outsider like an insider, and Zacchaeus immediately acted like one. The story ends with Jesus's life purpose: "The Son of Man came to seek and to save the lost" (Luke 19:10). This is important.

How to Adopt Jesus's Purpose

It's natural for us to judge people by their lifestyles. But Jesus has an uncanny ability to see beyond people's performance. Those driven by money may have father issues. Those driven by sex may have abandonment issues. Those driven by adventure may be looking for the divine in his creation. The way we're living now isn't necessarily what we want; it may be all we know. Given the chance to meet Jesus, many would go out on a limb just to get a glimpse of what you now have.

What often keeps people from Jesus is not Jesus's opinion of them but Christians' assumptions about them. Is there someone at school, in the neighborhood, or on your team that you've avoided but Jesus would run to? Find your Zacchaeus. Invite him first to your home, then to your church. You may get rejected; Jesus certainly did from time to time. If we call Jesus our Lord, shouldn't we call the people he prioritized our friends?

Key Points

- Jesus came for all people but seems to have a special place in his heart for the marginalized.

- Jesus knows you and *still* loves you. In fact, he really, really likes you!

- Jesus doesn't just know you; he needs you. He has a purpose for your life, and it likely involves introducing someone in your circle to him.

This Week

❑ **Day 1 (Eyes):** As you read the essay, did anyone specific come to mind who in some way is like Zacchaeus in your life?

❑ **Day 2 (Ears):** Read Ecclesiastes 5:8–6:12 through the eyes of Zacchaeus. How would he have interpreted this passage?

❑ **Day 3 (Heart):** Read through Romans 1:16, 2 Timothy 1:7–8, and 1 Peter 3:15–16. While reading each passage, ask the Holy Spirit three questions: *What do you want me to feel? What do you want me to do? Whom do you want me to influence?*

❑ **Day 4 (Voice):** Discussion:
- Share a story of someone you know whose life was radically different after she met Jesus.
- Why do you think we're so uncomfortable with people who are different from us, especially if they're wealthy or famous?
- What could your church do to reach out to those we assume wouldn't be interested in Jesus?
- Whom in your circle might you be able to influence to follow Jesus?

❑ **Day 5 (Hands):** Invite your "Zacchaeus" to the next party you go to, specifically to introduce him or her to your other Christian friends.

8

Did Jesus Have a
Life Purpose? Part 2

Biblical Concept: Life Purpose
Read: Mark 10:32–45

One day, when I was twelve, I heard Dad have a deadly serious but short conversation on the phone with my mom. When he hung up, he told me and my two brothers, "Mom is coming home, and we are going upstairs to talk. When we come down, we'll let you know what's going on." Even though I had never seen my parents fight, something inside told me this was the end of their marriage and the end of my life as I knew it.

We all have life-altering moments like that. It could be a visit to the doctor, a knock on the door, or a conversation in a car. You just know a difficult season is ahead that will test your character. That's what was happening in Mark 10.

The Beginning of the End and
the End of the Beginning

Jesus was traveling toward Jerusalem, and his disciples were lagging behind. It's as if they knew something bad was about to happen. Suddenly Jesus spelled it out as clear as could be:

See, we are going up to Jerusalem, and the Son of Man will be delivered over to the chief priests and the scribes, and they will condemn him to death and deliver him over to the Gentiles. And they will mock him and spit on him, and flog him and kill him. And after three days he will rise. (verses 33–34)

The disciples are unable to respond to Jesus's revelation of his impending death even though he had already predicted it twice (Mark 8:31–37; 9:30–32). It wasn't something they wanted to talk about. The silence was finally broken by a question, totally unrelated. James and John, with the support of their mother (Matthew 20:20), came to Jesus with a request.

A Bold Power Play

These two boys had been with Jesus since the beginning. They weren't just apostles. Along with Peter, they were Jesus's closest friends. They decided to see whether they could use this friendship to their advantage. The group was approaching Jerusalem. James and John thought he was about to be coronated and they didn't have much time to make a move. So they asked Jesus a question that none of us would expect.

"Will you give us whatever we ask?" Who in his right mind would say yes? Jesus asked, "What do you have in mind?" They replied, "Grant us to sit, one at your right hand and one at your left, in your glory" (Mark 10:37). In other words, James and John wanted positions of power. That was a bold move. The other disciples were furious, not because of James and John's selfish request but because the two had beaten them to the punch. Jesus must have been frustrated. They were missing the point.

Jesus's Advice on Becoming Great

Jesus's advice is the most significant leadership lesson in history. It has taken Western culture nearly two thousand years to catch up. Notice, Jesus didn't rebuke them for seeking greatness. In fact, he told them *how* to be great. If you have a passion to be a leader, to make a difference, to find significance, that's not a moral flaw. Rather, it's a divine impulse put there by your Creator. God wants you to be great; he even explained how, then immediately modeled it.

In his own words, "You know that those who are considered rulers of the Gentiles lord it over them, and their great ones exercise authority over them" (verse 42). The two worldly rulers found in Mark's gospel are Herod and Pilate. Pilate knew Jesus was innocent, but when the Jewish leaders threatened to blackmail him (John 19:12), he gave in to their demands. *He was ruled by his desire to be seen as a ruler.* Likewise, Herod gave in to the shocking request of his young stepdaughter (Mark 6:21–28). After she danced for his guests, he promised her up to half his kingdom. She asked for the head of John the Baptist. Herod knew it was evil but gave in anyway. Why? *He was ruled by his desire to be seen as a ruler.*

Rulers are still ruled by their desire to be seen as rulers. Jesus taught a different path: "Whoever would be great among you must be your servant, and whoever would be first among you must be slave of all" (Mark 10:43–44). This is where Jesus completely redefined what it means to be great. Greatness isn't about the power you have. It's about using your power to help other people. It's what we now call servant leadership. Through the Cross, Jesus gave us the ultimate example of what greatness and servant leadership look like: "Even the Son of Man came not to be served but to serve, and to give his life as a ransom for many" (verse 45).

The cross of Jesus isn't just what he did for us. It's the model of the life he expects from us. This takes us back to Eden, when God called Adam and Eve to be caretakers of the garden (Genesis 1:28). He created the heavens and the earth and invited human beings to partner with him in creating the world. Though sin and brokenness are everywhere, our call to create a beautiful world is still the same. That's why Jesus's cross can't be the only cross in Christianity. The cross of Christ saved sinners. The cross of Christians saves society. When we carry the cross of servant leadership, we alleviate suffering in society. That's how we achieve true greatness— not only in the eyes of God but also in the presence of a watching world.

Key Points

- Jesus's disciples ignored his predictions of suffering, showing how difficult it is to accept servant leadership.

- Jesus never criticized James and John for wanting to be great. Rather, he told them how.

- Servant leadership is the most powerful way to build a life of significance.

This Week

☐ **Day 1 (Eyes):** Did this essay change how you view your own desire to be great?

☐ **Day 2 (Ears):** What principles of servant leadership can you glean from Joshua 1, particularly since Joshua is the Hebrew name for Jesus?

☐ **Day 3 (Heart):** Think about the following passages, and ask how they reinforce Jesus's teaching on servant leadership: 1 Corinthians 9:19, 2 Corinthians 4:5, and 1 Peter 5:2–3.

☐ **Day 4 (Voice):** Discussion:

- Who is the best leader you've ever personally observed? Why?
- Jesus redefined greatness. Does his definition seem realistic in your world?
- Share about a time when you practiced servant leadership. What was the result?
- In what situations is it most difficult for you to humble yourself to serve? Why do you think it's hard for you to serve those people or in those ways?

☐ **Day 5 (Hands):** Do one thing this week for someone else that is uncomfortably humbling for you.

9

How Do I Recognize God's Call on My Life?

Biblical Concept: Calling
Read: Luke 5:1–11

I was sixteen at summer camp. With girls at campfires and buddies at lunch, my brain was pretty much at capacity. Still, I clearly heard God say, *Wouldn't you rather heal souls than brains?* (He knew I wanted to be a brain surgeon.) I thought my answer was clear: *No.* The Spirit persisted—for days. Frustrated, I finally said, *I've given you 95 percent of my life. All I'm asking for is my own career.* I swear I heard the Holy Spirit humph, then ask, *Aren't you glad Jesus didn't give* you *95 percent?* That wrecked me!

In desperation I gave in: *All right. I'll preach.* Miraculously, from that moment to this day, I've wanted to do nothing else. That's my story. Yours will be different. Just so we're clear, I'm not talking about the call to come to Christ. That's about salvation. This call is about service. How can we use the gifts God gave us to make Jesus famous?

It's Bigger than a Boat

The story takes place on the north shore of the Sea of Galilee. It's the biggest lake in the country and an essential source of food and water.

Jesus's popularity was rising, as was his opposition. Crowds were everywhere. A few local fishermen were on the shore, fixing their nets after a frustrating night of fishing. Jesus borrowed Peter's boat, pushed off from shore, and turned it into an amphitheater.

After his sermon, Jesus turned to Peter and said, "Put out into the deep and let down your nets for a catch" (Luke 5:4). What a dumb idea! It was the wrong time of day to fish, and they had already come up empty that night. You can imagine Peter thinking, *Lord, you're a great preacher, but you obviously know nothing about fishing. You do you and leave fishing to me.*

Fortunately, what Peter might have been thinking wasn't what he said: "Master, we toiled all night and took nothing! But at your word I will let down the nets" (verse 5). "At your word" is the right response for Peter and for us. As best as we can tell, Peter met Jesus about nine months earlier. He had witnessed enough to know that Jesus never ceases to surprise you.

So Peter rowed backward into the deep and let down his nets. As if on cue, the fish raced into the nets, threatening to drag the boat to the bottom of the lake. Peter frantically called to James and John, who jumped into their boat and hurried to help bring in the catch.

Appropriate Response

One would think the fishermen, filled with excitement, would celebrate. This catch would give them bragging rights for years to come. The blessing, however, was almost too much to handle. James and John arrived with their boat. As they hauled in the nets, the fish just kept coming. They realized this could *drown* them. It was then that Peter understood that the person and power in his boat were no joke. Jesus is the living Lord.

Peter fell to his knees, waist deep in a squirming pile of fish, and cried, "Depart from me, for I am a sinful man, O Lord" (verse 8). When you meet Jesus—I mean really encounter the authentic Christ—it will undo you.

Perhaps you've had a similar awakening. If so, you may recognize the coming call: "Do not be afraid; from now on you will be catching men" (verse 10). Luke used a very interesting word for "catch." It means "to take live captives."

Unfortunately, many people have been snagged by Satan. They've been lured away from God and hooked and are now desperate for freedom. Jesus sends all his disciples (you too) on a search-and-rescue mission for POWs—live captives—of a spiritual war. There's nothing more important in all the world. The fishermen "left everything and followed him" (verse 11). What about you? Can you hear his call?

Practical Advice on Hearing God's Call

If you're a Christian, you have a call. Not just a call to salvation, but a call to service. The Spirit of God has given you spiritual gifts because he wants to love someone else through you. Your gift may be something that came miraculously after conversion or a talent given to you at birth. It becomes a *spiritual* gift when you give it back to the Holy Spirit in service.

You may say, "I have nothing to offer." Not true. Doubt yourself all you want, but don't doubt the Spirit of God. Don't doubt Jesus, who can enter your boat and do something transformational. Here are four principles to help you hear God's call:

1. God is calling you. If you listen, you'll hear him ask for both your ability and your availability.
2. He asks some people to give up their occupations; he asks others to give over their occupations. Either way, we are all called to be Jesus's representatives where we live, work, and play.
3. Often God's call comes through others. You may not hear a divine voice or sense an internal prompting. His call may come through a parent, a coach, or a pastor. It's often God speaking when someone says something like "You're incredibly observant of others' feelings." Or "You have a natural gift of leadership." Or "Could you help your peer develop this skill?"

4. Asking Jesus to leave you alone is pointless. He's more patient and persistent than you can imagine. So you might as well begin today to find and fulfill his call on your life.

Key Points

- God calls some people to give up their occupations and others to give over their occupations, but all are called to rescue Satan's captives and draw people to Jesus.

- Jesus enters your boat—your culture and community—and overwhelms your expectations.

- God may call you personally or even miraculously. Most often, however, his call comes through others who speak God's truth to you.

This Week

❑ **Day 1 (Eyes):** After reading the essay, are you able to put into words what God has called you to do?

❑ **Day 2 (Ears):** First Samuel 3 describes God's call on Samuel's life. What lessons can you draw from this passage about hearing God's call on your life?

❑ **Day 3 (Heart):** Think about the following verses, and ask how they define or describe your call: 2 Corinthians 5:20, 1 Peter 2:9–10, and 1 Peter 4:10–11.

❑ **Day 4 (Voice):** Discussion:
- When you think of a person who is called by God, what or who comes to mind?
- Share about a time when you think God was speaking to you. Do you think God ever calls and we don't hear him or we refuse to respond? What would keep a person from hearing God's voice?
- What are some of the ways God could speak to us (such as sermons, books, music, nature, parents, etc.)?
- Go around the circle, and tell others what you see in them or how they could draw people to Jesus by using their gifts, resources, and abilities.

❑ **Day 5 (Hands):** Write a mission statement for your life. How will you use what God has put in your hands to lead people to Jesus?

10

How Do You Get into Jesus's Inner Circle?

Biblical Concept: Family
Read: Mark 3:31–35

Belonging is a universal human longing, and rejection is especially painful. I remember feeling this on the playground as a skinny kid trying to get picked for kickball. In middle school it was at the dance. In high school it was not making the varsity team. In college it was not getting scholarships.

Perhaps that's why this question is so uncomfortable: How do you get into Jesus's inner circle? Most people expect God to treat everyone the same but probably secretly doubt that he will. So it's fair to ask, "Why does God give priority to certain people?" And more importantly, "Am I one of them?" Let's turn to Mark 3:31–35 to find out.

Blood Is Not Thicker than Water

The old saying "Blood is thicker than water" is a claim that family trumps every other allegiance. Jesus rejected this notion in this short story that has huge implications. Mark 3:31–32 says, "His mother and his brothers came, and standing outside they sent to him and called him. And a crowd was sitting around him, and they said to him, 'Your mother and your brothers are outside, seeking you.'" In Jesus's day, family ties were much stronger than ours usually are. In the West, individual rights and freedoms are the primary focus. But in the Middle East, your identity comes from family, occupation, and location.

Jesus's life broke many of his cultural norms, but not because he was a Western individualist. Rather, he was prioritizing his heavenly Father over his earthly mother. After his baptism, Jesus didn't move back home to Nazareth. Instead, he moved his movement to Capernaum, where many of his disciples were from: James, John, Peter, Andrew, and Matthew. Now he was sitting in a home (likely Peter's), teaching his chosen few.

Jesus walked with them, sat in a circle and taught them, and gathered at a table and ate with them. That sounds normal to us, even polite. However, people in those days didn't go out to eat to get to know someone. Meals were markers for insiders—mostly family. To eat with others and ignore your own family was culturally unacceptable. As we'll see, Jesus did exactly this. But why?

Literary Sandwiches

Think of Mark's story as a literary sandwich. You stack two similar stories like two pieces of bread. Then you slip a story in the middle that's like the meat. The meaning of the middle story flavors how you're supposed to read the outer stories. This is a clever device, which Mark used several times in his gospel (4:1–20; 5:21–43; 11:12–25; 14:1–11; 14:53–72).

Notice that Mark 3:20–21 and 3:31–35 are about Jesus's family (that's the bread of the sandwich). Between these two stories is the famous discussion about Jesus casting out demons (the meat): "The scribes who came down from Jerusalem were saying, 'He is possessed by Beelzebul,' and 'by the prince of demons he casts out the demons'" (verse 22). The accusation by the scribes that he was possessed by a demon and the accusation by his family, "He is *out of his mind*" (verse 21), are different ways of saying the exact same thing. While our culture attributes mental illness to psychological problems, their worldview attributed mental illness to spiritual warfare.

Mark was sending a clear message: Jesus's family was on the same side as his opposition. They all believed him to be deceived by the devil. That made them outsiders to Jesus's movement, not insiders. The family was dead set on reining him in, which forced Jesus to force them out.

Getting into Jesus's Inner Circle

The story tells us how insiders became outsiders. Jesus's family treated him in the same way as his enemies. They attributed his power to dark forces and assumed he was heading in the wrong spiritual direction. They even tried to physically take hold of him as the soldiers did when they arrested him.

The story also tells us how outsiders became insiders. Some of the people who came in verse 8 were from Tyre and Sidon—ancient enemies of Israel. Outsiders were welcomed into the Jesus movement. They had a place at his table. When his family knocked at the door, he ignored them in favor of those who showed loyalty. Jesus said, " 'Who are my mother and my brothers?' And looking about at those who sat around him, he said, 'Here are my mother and my brothers! For whoever does the will of God, he is my brother and sister and mother' " (verses 33–35).

This story is great news, especially to those who've felt left out. The inner circle is reserved for those who respond to Jesus and live according to God's Word. He gives unprecedented access to those who give unqualified obedience to God's will. Anyone is welcome. Jesus's inner circle is determined not by where you came from but by where you're headed. You can be a part of Jesus's inner circle, and it turns out to be more your decision than his. He's already chosen you.

Key Points

- Blood is *not* thicker than water, at least according to Jesus.

- Mark's story shows how Jesus's family was more similar to his enemies than to his disciples.

- To Jesus, insiders are those who prioritize their heavenly Father over their earthly families.

This Week

❏ **Day 1 (Eyes):** As you read the essay, what was one thing about this story that stuck out to you and might have caused you to think differently about Jesus and his inner circle?

❏ **Day 2 (Ears):** Read Isaiah 49. Look for clues as to how Jesus might have read this chapter in light of his own ministry. If he was to restore Israel, what would he do for other nations?

❏ **Day 3 (Heart):** Think about 1 Corinthians 12:13, Ephesians 2:14, and Colossians 3:11. Rewrite these verses for your own context—what groups have been or should be brought together in your local church?

❏ **Day 4 (Voice):** Discussion:

- Share about a time when you felt special because you were in someone's inner circle. What specifically made you feel valued?
- Have you ever said, "That's not fair"? What was it about, and how did your parent, teacher, or coach respond?
- Have you had an experience in church that made you feel like you didn't belong? What made you feel that way?
- Are we sending messages verbally or nonverbally that could make people feel like they don't belong in Jesus's inner circle? What could we do to be more open, especially in our smaller groups?

❏ **Day 5 (Hands):** Find a friend who doesn't attend any church and ask her, "If you ever decided to go to church, what would make you feel like you were welcome there?"

11

Does My Past Determine My Future?

Biblical Concept: Shame
Read: Luke 7:36–50

One of my most memorable moments preaching was in Oronogo, Missouri. The text was Romans 8:1: "There is therefore now no condemnation for those who are in Christ Jesus." I challenged the audience to write down a sin they had been holding against themselves, walk to the front, and slip the paper into a fifty-gallon trash can. From a group of nine hundred, I expected a dozen or so to come forward. I was *way* off. Nearly every person had something to let go of.

People stood in line to release their sin and shame. I prayed a few feet away: *Lord, thank you for using me to release these people from self-bondage.*

The Holy Spirit said, *What about you?*

I asked, *What do you mean?* But I knew what he meant. For more than a decade, I had held secret shame from a past sin. I didn't want to admit that in front of the crowd I had just preached to. Ultimately, though, I feared God's opinion more than theirs. So I got in line with everyone else and released what I had held against myself for so long.

Trust me when I say I know the power of being released from shame. I'm just like the woman in this story.

Table, Tears, and Tyranny

The scene is set in the dining room of Simon the Pharisee. Jesus was his "honored" guest. The elite of the community joined them, reclining on cushions. The table was low to the ground, maybe six inches high, and U-shaped.

In those days, locals could come into the courtyards of prominent homes like this to conduct business and handle community affairs. The more impressed these people were with the meal, the more honor Simon gained in the community.

One of the locals was a woman with a bad reputation. We can't know for sure, but there's reason to believe that this woman was a prostitute. Just so we're clear, that isn't any little girl's dream. Most of the time, women are forced into sex trafficking because of abuse or financial difficulty. This nameless woman came in and collapsed at Jesus's feet.

Simon recoiled in a fetal position. Jesus watched intently as her tears rained down on his feet. Perhaps instinctively, she cleaned up the mess with the only thing available: her hair—which would be a big deal for women. After wiping his feet clean, she opened a jar of ointment and proceeded to rub its expensive contents on his feet. (From John 12:5, we know that a pint of this stuff was worth a year's wages.)

Simon thought to himself, "If this man were a prophet, he would have known who and what sort of woman this is who is touching him, for she is a sinner" (Luke 7:39). Jesus read his mind: "Simon, I have something to say to you." Simon answered with sarcastic respect, "Say it, Teacher" (verse 40).

What Love Looks Like

Jesus replied with a story. The main character was a moneylender. One guy owed him two years' salary (five hundred denarii). The second guy owed him a fraction of that: fifty denarii. Neither could pay him back. But this moneylender forgave both debts (a crazy thought). "Which of them will love him more?" Jesus asked (verse 42). "The one, I suppose, for whom he cancelled the larger debt," Simon said (verse 43). Exactly!

What happened next is stunning. Jesus turned and looked at the woman but spoke to Simon. "Do you see this woman? I entered your house; you gave me no water for my feet, but she has wet my feet with her tears and wiped them with her hair. You gave me no kiss, but from the time I came in she has not ceased to kiss my feet. You did not anoint my head with oil, but she has anointed my feet with ointment. Therefore I tell you, her sins, which are many, are forgiven—for she loved much. But he who is forgiven little, loves little" (verses 44–47).

Simon had neglected every common courtesy. He didn't wash Jesus's feet—a kindness toward guests who had walked on dusty roads in sandals. This woman, however, washed Jesus's feet with tears. Simon didn't greet Jesus with a kiss on each cheek. The woman, on the other hand, hadn't yet stopped kissing his feet. Simon didn't put a tablespoon of olive oil on Jesus's head, which was a thing. In contrast, she rubbed costly ointment on Jesus's feet.

It's obvious who loved Jesus more. It's equally obvious why: her sins had been forgiven. Without words, she demonstrated true repentance. Which is why Jesus publicly declared her spiritual debt canceled.

The Shattering of Shame

Jesus looked at the woman and told her, "Your sins are forgiven. . . . Your faith has saved you; go in peace" (verses 48, 50). Let that sink into your soul. It's time to release your shame to Jesus. You don't need more words or sacrifices. You don't need to beat yourself up or apologize again and again. If you've repented of your sin, confessed it to God, and made amends as best you can, you can let it go. You are free. Fully. Finally.

We don't know for sure who this woman was, but she may well have been Mary Magdalene, who is introduced in the very next passage (Luke 8:1–3). If this woman wasn't Mary, she was someone very much like her. The Bible says Mary had seven demons before meeting Jesus (verse 2).

Clearly, she was a woman with a past. Yet all four Gospels identify Mary Magdalene as the first witness to the Resurrection. She's a great example of someone whose past didn't determine her future. Your future can be unchained from your past if you can correctly answer this one question: How much do you love Jesus?

Key Points

- Religious leaders sometimes justify themselves by comparing their "righteousness" with others' sinfulness.

- Jesus runs toward sinners, not away from them.

- Jesus doesn't want you carrying a burden of shame. He has declared your debt paid in full.

This Week

☐ **Day I (Eyes):** After reading the essay, do you need to release some sin or regret you've been holding against yourself?

☐ **Day 2 (Ears):** Read Moses's story in Exodus 2:11–4:17. He was the founder of the Jewish nation, yet he began as a fugitive. What lessons does this hold for you about getting past your past?

☐ **Day 3 (Heart):** Think about Romans 8:1, 1 Timothy 1:15, and 1 John 1:9. How does each verse help you answer the question, "Does my past determine my future?"

☐ **Day 4 (Voice):** Discussion:
- Share a story of someone you know who radically turned his life around.
- "Sin is not just what you do but what was done to you." In other words, past abuse often leads to poor choices in the future. How have you seen that played out?
- What happens to your body, mind, and emotions when you hold on to the shame of sin?
- What are some helpful ways of releasing guilt and shame? Feel free to use the verses listed in day 3 to get some ideas.

☐ **Day 5 (Hands):** Schedule a time with God this week. Write down any sin you're still holding against yourself. Practice 1 John 1:9. Claim Romans 8:1. Destroy the paper.

12

Who Are Social Influencers for Jesus? Part I

Biblical Concept: Influence
Read: John 3:1–21

Have you ever had a flight canceled in the airport? It's extremely frustrating. On one such occasion, a customer thought he was more special than the rest. He pushed past the others in line and growled at the attendant, "Do you know who I am? *Do you know who I am?*" Unfazed, the attendant got on the microphone. "Ladies and gentlemen, if anyone has lost an adult male in your party, he is at the counter and apparently does not know who he is." The crowd cheered. The "important" man sheepishly went to the back of the line. In a sense, the same thing is about to happen in this text.

In the Dark of Night

Nicodemus was the most influential person Jesus had met up to that point. He sat on Israel's highest court, called the Sanhedrin. It had only seventy-one members, making Nicodemus elite. As a Pharisee, he was a firm defender of conservative Judaism. Unlike his colleagues, however, he liked Jesus. He said, "Rabbi, we know that you are a teacher come from

God, for no one can do these signs that you do unless God is with him" (John 3:2). That's huge. He admitted that Jesus was a rabbi even though Jesus had none of Nicodemus's formal education. He affirmed that Jesus's miracles were legitimate. He was seriously considering whether Jesus was the Messiah and how he might use his influence to promote Jesus's ministry.

Nicodemus's name could go a long way in opening doors, breaking down barriers, and gaining goodwill among the people. So, why didn't Jesus welcome him with open arms? Many pastors would have lunged at Nicodemus the second he set foot in the building.

There are several clues. First, Nicodemus came to Jesus at night. It wasn't because Nicodemus was busy during the day. Something deeper was going on here. It appears that he didn't want his affinity for Jesus to become public.

Furthermore, *night, dark,* and *darkness* occur thirteen times in the book of John (1:5; 3:2, 19; 6:17; 8:12; 9:4; 11:10; 12:35, 46; 13:30; 19:39; 20:1; 21:3). Most of these references are metaphors for spiritual darkness. *Night* seems to describe Nicodemus's spiritual condition as much as the time frame (3:2, 19).

Second, Nicodemus's confession of Jesus fell short. In the first chapter of John, Jesus had been declared "the Word," "Lamb of God," "Son of God," "Messiah," and "King of Israel" (verses 1, 29, 34, 41, 49). The best Nicodemus could muster was "Rabbi." Was it honorable? Yes. Was it sufficient? Not even close.

There's a third clue. Nicodemus was pretty engaged at first (3:1–8). But Jesus told this Sanhedrin superstar that his credentials didn't matter. He had to come into the kingdom at ground level like everyone else: "Truly, truly, I say to you, unless one is born again he cannot see the kingdom of God" (verse 3). When he was called to humility, Nicodemus checked out.

What Do You Do with Nicodemus?

Two other times Nicodemus would come to Jesus's defense. In John 7, Jesus was getting railroaded. Nicodemus defended his right to a fair trial: "Does our law judge a man without first giving him a hearing and learning what he does?" (verse 51). His colleagues reacted with anger: "Are you from Galilee too? Search and see that no prophet arises from Galilee" (verse 52). You know what Nicodemus said next? Nothing! Absolutely nothing.

We meet Nicodemus one final time, in John 19:39. He joined Joseph of Arimathea, providing an honorable burial for Jesus. That's good, right? Well, yes, but it's hardly enough. Joseph is identified as a secret disciple of Jesus. That's the problem for both Joseph and Nicodemus. They wanted to be close to Jesus without going public. Sorry—that's not an option. You can't have a personal relationship without public acknowledgment. That's not just true for Jesus; it's a relational reality. Would you date someone who wasn't willing to tell others about you? True devotion in discipleship or any other relationship requires declaration. As William Barclay observed, "Discipleship kills the secrecy or the secrecy kills . . . discipleship."[1] If you want to be a secret disciple, the best you can hope for is what Nicodemus achieved. He became the caretaker of Jesus's corpse.

Many so-called disciples are like Nicodemus. They imagine that Jesus is fortunate to have them. After all, they can promote his agenda, even if they do it on their own terms. They want the benefits of being a disciple without the cost. Based on this encounter, that doesn't end well. Jesus's unparalleled sacrifice demands absolute devotion. The verse that follows on the heels of this meeting has rightly become the most famous statement in all of Scripture: "God so loved the world, that he gave his only Son, that whoever believes in him should not perish but have eternal life" (John 3:16).

The lesson is clear: in the kingdom of God, your power is irrelevant; your faith is everything. Jesus isn't impressed with how far you can puff out your chest; he's impressed with the heart inside the chest. Furthermore, he doesn't need your status or influence to further his agenda. So, whom does Jesus prioritize? We will have to await the next chapter for the full answer. For now, we can say with certainty, it's *not* Nicodemus. There's nothing wrong with having influence. It just doesn't give you a firm foundation for authentic discipleship. Jesus deserves more. Jesus demands more.

Key Points

- Nicodemus, despite all his credentials, failed to follow Jesus.

- Jesus demands that we all be born again, humbling ourselves and putting our faith in him.

- Trying to be a disciple secretly doesn't work in relation to Jesus. His sacrifice demands our total allegiance.

This Week

❏ **Day 1 (Eyes):** Before reading the essay, had you ever thought that some people had a higher standing with God because of their titles, their leadership roles, or some other public recognition?

❏ **Day 2 (Ears):** Read 1 Samuel 10:9–27 and 13:1–15. What similarities do you see between the life of Saul and the life of Nicodemus?

❏ **Day 3 (Heart):** Think about Acts 10:34, Romans 2:11, and James 2:1–7. Who are God's favorites?

❏ **Day 4 (Voice):** Discussion:

- When you think of the term *religious person,* who comes to mind? You can either describe a specific person or list the characteristics of such a person.
- What does it mean to be born again? We're asking about the personal experience, not the theological definition.
- What keeps people in general or you specifically from giving your life to Jesus?
- In what areas of your life have you tried to be a secret disciple? Have you ever been embarrassed about your faith or afraid to share it openly?

❏ **Day 5 (Hands):** Do one simple thing or have one simple conversation to make your commitment to Jesus more visible. It could be placing a Bible on your desk, using a scripture as your phone's wallpaper, or saying to a friend, "Have I ever told you why I go to church?"

13

Who Are Social Influencers for Jesus? Part 2

Biblical Concept: Influence
Read: John 4:4–42

In the previous lesson, we met Nicodemus. He held such promise as a social influencer. Yet Jesus showed no interest in seeking his favor. In this lesson, we see the complete opposite. There was a woman at a well. No one was interested in her *except* Jesus. She was the kind of person you ghost when she pops up on your phone. Yet she wound up being Jesus's greatest advocate! It's worth leaning in to eavesdrop on their conversation.

A Well, a Woman, and Water

Our story begins with a simple statement: "He *had* to pass through Samaria" (John 4:4). But Jesus didn't *have* to go through Samaria because of geography. In fact, most Jews went around Samaria, following the Jordan River up to Galilee. Rather, Jesus *had* to talk to this Samaritan woman. He wasn't about to let racial tensions or geographical barriers keep him from this conversation.

It may seem normal today to cross ethnic and gender lines; in Jesus's day, it was forbidden. Men weren't supposed to talk with women. And Jews weren't supposed to interact with Samaritans. Jesus was breaking barriers that had existed for hundreds of years! Samaritans were descendants of the ten northern tribes of Israel, the remnant left after the rich people were carted off to captivity in Assyria. To repopulate the area, the Assyrians imported other people groups, who then intermarried with the locals. Consequently, the Jews considered their Samaritan cousins polluted. To make matters worse, the Samaritans had an alternative temple on Mount Gerizim and an altered version of the Old Testament that offended Jews.

"He came to a town of Samaria called Sychar, near the field that Jacob had given to his son Joseph. Jacob's well was there; so Jesus, wearied as he was from his journey, was sitting beside the well. It was about the sixth hour" (verses 5–6). It was noon—that is, the sixth hour after sunrise. Why hadn't this woman come to the well in the early morning with all the other women of the village? It becomes clear when we learn she'd had five husbands and now lived with a man she wasn't married to. She was the scandal of the community, used by men and rejected by women. The well was small. She couldn't avoid Jesus, especially when he broke the silence, saying, "Give me a drink" (verse 7).

Shocked, she asked, "How is it that you, a Jew, ask for a drink from me, a woman of Samaria?" (verse 9). Jesus answered, "If you knew the gift of God, and who it is that is saying to you, 'Give me a drink,' you would have asked him, and he would have given you living water" (verse 10).

"Living water?" she said skeptically. "Prove it!" Jesus replied, "Sure . . . as soon as you call your husband." Uh-oh. She didn't have a husband. She could muster only three words (in Greek): "Husband don't have."

"That's right," Jesus revealed: "You've had five, and the man you're with now isn't your husband." He now had her undivided attention. "Sir," she said, "I perceive that you are a prophet" (verse 19). Because she was uncomfortable, she tried to change the subject.

Jesus wouldn't be deterred. He drove the conversation back to himself, not as an egomaniac but as the Savior. We would do well to follow his lead. Often when you talk to your friends about faith, they'll bring up topics like evolution or the problem of pain to prove why it's hard to believe. Focus on Jesus. When you get Jesus right, little else matters. Until you get him right, nothing else matters.

The Villain Becomes the Hero

She raced to town and said, "Come, see a man who told me all that I ever did. Can this be the Christ?" (verse 29). In the original language, her question assumed a "No." We might ask it like this: "He couldn't be the Messiah, could he?" Knowing her reputation, the locals were likely to disagree with her, regardless of what she said. But out of curiosity, they went out in droves to see the man at the well.

When they came to Jesus, he broke the barriers of the Samaritans and overturned the expectations of his followers. He saw the Samaritans as children of God, not enemies of Israel. Perhaps that's why they were so open to his teaching. His message was simply and exclusively this: I am the promised Messiah.

It was too good to be true! They believed in Jesus. In the end, they said to the woman, "We have heard for ourselves, and we know that this is indeed the Savior of the world" (verse 42). *Savior of the world* was a common title for the emperor. It was the caption on many coins in the Roman world. That puts this confession above any Jesus had heard so far, and it came from outsiders.

So, here's the point. Nicodemus should have influenced people toward Jesus, but he never did. The woman, on the other hand, went down in biblical history as the single most effective evangelist in the Gospels. Nicodemus was a Jew; she was a Samaritan. He was a man; she was a woman. He was a famous Sanhedrin lawyer; she had a bad reputation. *Yet* Nicodemus came to Jesus in the darkness of night, while Jesus "needed" to go to the woman in the noonday light. Nicodemus was commanded to be reborn in water; she was offered living water. Nicodemus's countrymen crucified Jesus; hers hailed him as the Savior of the world.

We're now prepared to answer this question: Who are social influencers for Jesus? You tell me.

Key Points

- The Samaritan woman was the least likely person to influence others for Jesus, yet she did. You can too.

- Jesus didn't avoid her past or judge her for it. Rather, he allowed her to use all of who she was to influence others to come to him.

- The discussion Jesus wants to have with us and wants us to have with others is not about theology but about his identity as the Savior of the world.

This Week

❑ **Day 1 (Eyes):** After reading the essay, what influence do you think you could have for Jesus?

❑ **Day 2 (Ears):** Second Kings 6:24–7:20 tells another incredible story that happened in Samaria. Can you find parallel spiritual lessons between the two stories?

❑ **Day 3 (Heart):** Think about your influence for Jesus in light of Romans 1:16, 1 Corinthians 1:20, and 1 Corinthians 3:18–19.

❑ **Day 4 (Voice):** Discussion:
- Other than Jesus, who are some of the most influential people in history?
- Have you ever known someone who was severely overrated or underrated? Perhaps an athlete or pop star?
- What was it about Nicodemus that made him so ineffective as a follower? Why was the Samaritan woman so influential?
- What do you think would allow you to be more influential for Jesus?

❑ **Day 5 (Hands):** On a three-by-five card, write down one person you want to influence for Jesus and one specific step you could encourage that person to take toward him.

Section 2

The Power of Jesus

Next we'll look at Jesus's miracles. In one sense, they are **wonders** that make us say, "Wow, look at how powerful he is." In another sense, they are **signs** that make us say, "Ahhh, so that's what he wants us to do." And then there are **claims** to which we say, "Oh snap, that's gonna ruffle some feathers." His miracles point to both his identity and his ultimate purpose.

Wonders: chapters 14–17
Signs: chapters 18–22
Claims: chapters 23–26

14

Is Christianity Boring?

Biblical Concept: Celebration
Read: John 2:1–12

For many reasons, I'm glad I grew up in church. There I found my faith, went on my first mission trip, and got my first kiss (our Sunday school teacher wondered where we were). However, the music back then was out of a songbook called a hymnal and was accompanied by the drone of an organ. The preacher spoke for approximately forty-five minutes, but it felt like a day and a half. That was church as I knew it. So don't criticize me for asking, "Is Christianity boring?" It may seem so—even today. However, after this story from the life of Jesus, you may answer differently.

The Wedding at Cana

Weddings in our day tend to be less than an hour. If you're lucky, there's a meal at the reception to go with the cake. For the Jews, however, a wedding was a blowout bash, lasting up to seven days. The difference is that a Jewish marriage was an alliance between two families, not just a husband and wife. The groom was showing his ability to provide for the bride's family. If he failed at the wedding, it was a massive problem since he didn't meet the legal obligation that the dowry created. The celebration placed a lot of pressure on the groom.

At this wedding, the family had asked Jesus's mother, Mary, to supervise the food services in Cana, about six miles from Nazareth. Both were small villages, and the families were deeply connected. It wasn't just an honor for Mary; it was a heavy obligation. She had to make sure the food and wine would stretch across the entire celebration. If she pulled it off, her influence would increase. This was even more important since it appears that her husband, Joseph, was deceased. He's never mentioned in the present tense after Jesus turned twelve. If that was the case, Mary, as a widow, had very few opportunities to improve her social standing. This was a chance she couldn't afford to lose.

Jesus had been invited as well. His presence was a big deal for the families. He was like a celebrity. For the past several months, he'd been kicking off his career, making a name for himself and attracting followers. Jesus's entourage added to the wedding. It also, however, put pressure on the dwindling supply of food and wine. In fact, it might have been this thirsty band that sucked the wine cellar dry.

Mary had a problem. She called on Jesus for the solution, telling him, "They have no wine" (John 2:3). It's doubtful that she expected him to do a miracle. Rather, she probably thought he would help pay for more wine.

His response must have taken her breath away: "Woman, what does this have to do with me?" (verse 4). He didn't call her "Mom" or "Mother." Just "Woman." Now, that wasn't an insult, but it was far from a promising reply. Then when he asked her why she was involving him, she must have thought, *Well, because I'm your mother!* Culturally she had every right to expect him to help her. But at this very time God was calling Jesus to his messianic career.

Now Jesus had a problem. Take care of his earthly mother or follow his heavenly Father? Perhaps that's why Jesus added, "My hour has not yet come" (verse 4). Throughout John's gospel, *hour* is a metaphor for Jesus's suffering (4:21, 23; 5:25, 28; 7:30; 8:20; 12:23, 27; 13:1; 16:25, 32; 17:1).

It was also a clear reference to God's call over and above Mary's request. So, as only Jesus could do, he helped his earthly mother while following his heavenly Father.

The Meaning of the Miracle

Mary somehow sensed that Jesus was about to do something big. And he did! There were six stone jars that could hold twenty to thirty gallons each. That's 120 to 180 gallons. The servants filled the jars to the top, then took a sample to the master of ceremonies. He was astounded at the taste test: "Everyone serves the good wine first, and when people have drunk freely, then the poor wine. But you have kept the good wine until now" (John 2:10). Now, there's a wedding gift worth remembering: 180 gallons of wine is a blessing you can bathe in!

What does this miracle mean? Well, John never called it a miracle; he called it a sign. Miracles make you say, "Wow." Signs make you say, "Oooooh." The seven signs of John are like chapters in a story. The whole story is how to become a fully devoted follower of Jesus.

#	Text	Miracle	Lesson
1	2:1–11	Water to wine	You are invited to a celebration.
2	4:46–54	Official's son	You have to come with faith.
3	5:1–15	Lame man	You come to Jesus not for healing but for him.
4	6:1–15	Feeding five thousand	Jesus is your sustenance.
5	6:16–21	Walking on water	Jesus overcomes chaos.
6	9:1–41	Blind man	Jesus gives you sight.
7	11:1–44	Lazarus	Jesus restores your life.

Jesus strengthens us, overcomes our chaos, gives us sight, and raises us from the dead. But our journey with him begins with an invitation to a wedding—a celebration *and* a lifelong commitment. Jesus is the groom; the church is the bride (Ephesians 5:22–33). It all ends with a wedding too. When Jesus returns, the first party in eternity will be the wedding supper of the Lamb:

> I heard what seemed to be the voice of a great multitude, like the roar of many waters and like the sound of mighty peals of thunder, crying out,
>
> "Hallelujah!
> For the Lord our God
>   the Almighty reigns.
> Let us rejoice and exult
>   and give him the glory,
> for the marriage of the Lamb has come,
>   and his Bride has made herself ready." (Revelation 19:6–7)

So, let me ask again, "Is Christianity boring?" Hardly.

Key Points

- Following Jesus is more about celebration than sacrifice.
- All the signs of John point to our own journeys with Jesus.
- Our journeys with Jesus begin and end with a wedding.

This Week

❑ **Day 1 (Eyes):** After reading the essay, answer this question: Have you seen church more as a celebration or as an obligation?

❑ **Day 2 (Ears):** The Song of Solomon is a romantic love poem. Many of the earliest Christian leaders, however, read it as an allegory of Christ and the church. Try that. Read Song of Solomon 5, and see how it might describe your relationship with Christ.

❑ **Day 3 (Heart):** Think about 2 Corinthians 11:2, Ephesians 5:23, and Revelation 21:9. What do they say about our spiritual wedding?

❑ **Day 4 (Voice):** Discussion:
- Share your earliest memories of church. Your favorite memory in church. One time you got in trouble in church.
- What do you imagine your wedding will be like?
- Why do you think many people see church as boring or irrelevant?
- What could we do to change that perception?

❑ **Day 5 (Hands):** Ask a friend who doesn't go to church what would make it a place she might like to go.

15

Can Jesus Turn My Storm into a Story?

Biblical Concept: Chaos
Read: Mark 4:35–5:20

Today is tough for me. Our world is living through a pandemic, and our nation is experiencing social upheaval. On top of all that, I just received some tragic personal news. As I was typing, a dear friend of mine texted that he has stage IV cancer and has two weeks to live. Don't feel sorry for me. You have your own story, and most are more serious than mine. The question is whether Jesus can help us in the middle of our storms. This story is all about the "Yes."

Fear of a Storm

This is the second-longest recorded day in Jesus's life. Each of the following events builds on a single theme: fear. The disciples were afraid in a storm. The people from Gerasa were afraid of Jesus. A bleeding woman was afraid of being found out. Jairus was afraid his daughter would die. Only the Gerasenes got it right. Jesus is the only one we need fear. Once we fear Jesus, we can be fearless. Our focus here will be on the storm and the demon-possessed man.

While Jesus and the disciples were crossing the Lake of Galilee, "a great windstorm arose" (Mark 4:37). The rim of hills around the lake was about two thousand feet above the waterline. Storms would sweep down the hills and crash into the lake. This kind of storm had sunk many ships, instantly throwing fishing businesses like Peter's into bankruptcy. The disciples were afraid for their lives and livelihood. Meanwhile, Jesus was fast asleep. This frustrated the disciples: "Teacher, do you not care that we are perishing?" (verse 38). They wanted his help to bail out the boat. He had a better idea.

What Jesus did next isn't recommended. He stood up in the boat. (Of course, if you can walk on water, standing in a rowboat is less risky.) Then he rebuked the wind and waves. Jesus's command could be translated, "Shut up!" The wind and waves immediately obeyed. All creation is under his authority (John 1:1–4; Colossians 1:16–17; Hebrews 1:3).

The boys in the boat were dumbfounded. So was Jesus. He couldn't believe their unbelief: "Why are you so afraid? Have you still no faith?" (Mark 4:40). One of the few things that truly shocked Jesus was people's persistent unbelief (7:18; 8:17–18, 21, 32–33; 9:19). However, these disciples were getting a glimpse of his true identity: "Who then is this, that even the wind and the sea obey him?" (4:41). Fear of Jesus is a sign that you've seen him for who he really is.

Fear of a Savior

It was the middle of the night. They were cold, wet, and spooked. It was about to get worse. As they went ashore, a demoniac came bounding down from the cliffs. He was a well-known local who terrorized the villagers. He was homicidal, suicidal, buck naked, and very loud. He was also so freakishly strong that chains couldn't contain him. On the plateau high above stood a few spectators. They were pig herders on the night watch.

To their amazement, the demoniac came to a screeching halt at the feet of Jesus. He cried, "What have you to do with me, Jesus, Son of the Most High God? I adjure you by God, do not torment me" (Mark 5:7).

He knew Jesus had the authority to order the demons out. The demons begged Jesus to send them into the pigs. He did. The demons destroyed the pigs. Why? Because Satan's natural bent is to "steal and kill and destroy" (John 10:10).

The herdsmen raced off to town in the middle of the night. This was an emergency. The entire herd was wiped out! Some object to Jesus destroying private property. However, humans always come before unclean animals. When the villagers arrived, the crazy streaker was clothed and in his right mind. Where did he get the clothes? Knowing Jesus, he probably gave the man the robe off his own back.

The locals pleaded with Jesus, "Go away. You frighten us." Note: Jesus is respectful. He won't force himself on any of us. If you demand that he leave, he probably will. Note, too, that when we meet Jesus, we have only two options: kneel before him as Lord or totally reject him. He is not, however, one we can casually ignore. He will be above all or nothing at all.

Faith of a Survivor

Meanwhile, the ex-demoniac begged Jesus to let him follow. Jesus said, "No." Instead, Jesus told him, "Go home to your friends and tell them how much the Lord has done for you, and how he has had mercy on you" (Mark 5:19). The man apparently did! The next time Jesus entered the area, he fed four thousand people (8:1–9). Where did they come from? Our best guess is one lone ex-demoniac shared his story with everyone he could.

Many of us can relate to the demoniac. When we experience a storm, our reaction is to run away or hide. Get a new start and perhaps a new identity. But Jesus had more in store for the demoniac, and he has more in store for you. Often our deepest pain becomes our highest platform. Your story may be the very thing that brings Jesus the greatest honor.

Key Points

- In the storm, Jesus proved to be more than his disciples ever imagined. He is, in fact, Creator God, with the power to order nature itself.

- Jesus values you above all else in his creation.

- Your story, as painful as it may be, has more potential to bring healing than your past ever had to bring destruction.

This Week

☐ **Day 1 (Eyes):** After reading the essay, think through one simple question: Are you more afraid of Jesus or the storm you face?

☐ **Day 2 (Ears):** Do a little detective work. Find the three verses in Psalm 2 that are quoted in the New Testament (a study Bible will help you locate them). Now look up each of those New Testament passages, and read two or three verses before and after the quotation of Psalm 2. What do these passages say about Jesus and his ability to take us through storms?

☐ **Day 3 (Heart):** Think about Ephesians 1:20–21, Colossians 2:9, and Revelation 1:17–18. According to these three passages, how do people underestimate who Jesus is?

☐ **Day 4 (Voice):** Discussion:
- Share the story of someone you know whose past pain has been a great encouragement or inspiration to you.
- If you're willing, share the most difficult thing you've ever had to go through.
- If a friend were going through a really difficult time, what advice or encouragement would you give to help your friend share his story to help others?
- Which piece of advice that you just heard do you need to implement to share your story with more people?

☐ **Day 5 (Hands):** This week, do what Jesus told the ex-demoniac to do: "Go home to your friends and tell them how much the Lord has done for you, and how he has had mercy on you" (Mark 5:19).

16

Can Jesus Provide for My Needs?

Biblical Concept: Provision
Read: Mark 6:31–52

Everyone seems to be busy these days. Homework, school, job, chores. Have you ever been so busy you forgot to eat? That's where I draw the line! But that's where Jesus was in this story: "Many were coming and going, and they had no leisure even to eat" (Mark 6:31). Jesus needed some time away with the twelve apostles to take a breath and regroup.

Jesus the Provider

They headed off to what the Bible describes as "a desolate place" (verse 31). The crowds saw him get into a boat, the kind that taxied people across the lake. They ran halfway around the lake—nine miles! When Jesus arrived, he was greeted by an anxious crowd five thousand strong. Well, actually, that was just the men. Counting women and children, it was likely three times that size.

I know how cranky I get when I'm overexposed to people's expectations. Yet Jesus, pressed by a restless crowd, "had compassion on them, because they were like *sheep without a shepherd*" (verse 34). In the Old

Testament, the first great shepherd was Moses, leading Israel in the desert. Other leaders likewise inherited the role of shepherd over God's people (Ezekiel 34:5, 23–24). None could live up to the ideal in Psalm 23: "The LORD is my shepherd" (verse 1). That is, until Jesus arrived: "When he saw the crowds, he had compassion for them, because they were harassed and helpless, like sheep without a shepherd" (Matthew 9:36).

Jesus responded with three actions. The order is important. First, he *taught* them (Mark 6:34). Their most immediate need was not physical but spiritual. Second, he *healed* them (Matthew 14:14), which was likely their immediate concern. Third, he *fed* them, which no one expected. All this is literal. But it's also spiritually symbolic of Jesus's entire ministry as the Messiah. It's so significant that this is the only miracle recorded in all four Gospels prior to the Resurrection.

The disciples suggested that Jesus "send them away to go into the surrounding countryside and villages and buy themselves something to eat" (Mark 6:36). The disciples were hungry and tired. Jesus, however, never missed a teachable moment: "You give them something to eat" (verse 37). Well, that's just ridiculous. Philip quickly calculated that "two hundred denarii [a year's salary!] worth of bread would not be enough for each of them to get a little" (John 6:7).

Peter's brother, Andrew, found a boy who was willing to share his lunch. Andrew was always taking someone to Jesus. He took Peter to Jesus in John 1:40–42 and a group of Greeks to him in John 12:20–22. This time, it was a kid with a lunchbox. "There is a boy here who has five barley loaves and two fish, but what are they for so many?" (John 6:9). Unfazed, Jesus ordered the troops to sit on the green grass.

Then, like a father, Jesus blessed the meal and passed the food. We really don't know whether he reproduced a mountain of loaves in one lump sum as he said "Amen" or whether he dispensed the loaves and fish like a Vegas blackjack dealer. Either way, it got everyone's attention.

The crowds were ready to make Jesus king! Jesus, however, dismissed them and ordered his disciples to get into the boat to go back across the lake. Jesus was to be a different kind of king. They must have been disappointed. They had been waiting for this moment, and Jesus killed the momentum.

Jesus the Protector

Jesus walked to the top of the mountain (actually a hill by our standards) and prayed late into the night. While he was praying, a storm pounded the boat in the middle of the lake. The disciples were about three and a half miles out. Jesus could see them from the mountain under the full moon around Passover. They were "making headway painfully" (Mark 6:48). It was the fourth watch of the night, which is three to six o'clock in the morning. They were wet, tired, cold, and frustrated. So Jesus walked out to them *on top of the water*! Freaky.

Mark made a strange observation: "He meant to pass by them" (verse 48). What in the world? Was he going to beat them to the other side so he could shout "Gotcha"? Funny, but no. This is a way of portraying Jesus as God. Jesus mysteriously identified himself as Yahweh when he said, "It is I" (verse 50). In Hebrew, it would be pronounced "Yahweh," the great "I Am." Then when Jesus got into the boat, "the wind ceased. And they were utterly astounded" (verse 51). God was on the water.

We have the advantage of twenty-twenty hindsight to see what they missed. The feeding of the five thousand portrays Jesus as Creator God, making something from nothing (Genesis 1:1). The walking on water portrays Jesus as the Spirit of God, hovering over the chaotic waters to bring order (verse 2). So, can Jesus provide for my needs?

Clearly, yes. The real question is, Have you made Jesus a big enough part of your life that you are now able to teach others, heal others, or feed others? Our responsibility is much like Andrew's: to lead people to Jesus.

That little boy gave his lunch. But it was more than enough for Jesus to bless the crowd. What you have in your hand right now is enough. Give it to Jesus and he can multiply it miraculously. He never *needs* what you have, but he can always *multiply* what you offer to meet needs in a way you never imagined.

Key Points

- Even when Jesus was exhausted, he found a way to teach, heal, and provide nourishment. This is a powerful model for us to follow.

- The feeding of the five thousand is symbolic of Jesus's entire ministry as the Messiah, which explains why all four Gospels tell the story.

- When Jesus fed the five thousand, he demonstrated his deity as described in Genesis 1:1. When he walked on water, he demonstrated his deity as described in Genesis 1:2.

This Week

☐ **Day 1 (Eyes):** After reading the essay, answer this question: Is there anyone you feel physically or spiritually responsible to care for?

☐ **Day 2 (Ears):** Read Exodus 16, the story of manna in the wilderness. What lessons or guidelines about manna are given in Exodus 16 that you could apply to your journey with Jesus?

☐ **Day 3 (Heart):** Think about Acts 20:28, 1 Peter 2:25, and Revelation 7:17. What do these verses say about Jesus as shepherd?

☐ **Day 4 (Voice):** Discussion:

- What's the busiest season you've ever been through? What sustained you through it?
- What individuals or groups would you describe as "sheep without a shepherd"? What could you do to lead or feed them?
- How should this teaching, healing, feeding model of Jesus's ministry shape the way you interact with people?
- Are you spiritually hungry right now? How are you receiving strength from Jesus? What does he do to meet your spiritual, physical, and emotional needs?

☐ **Day 5 (Hands):** Make the time this week to teach, heal, or feed someone either physically or spiritually.

17

Is Jesus Really Divine?

Biblical Concept: Divinity
Read: Mark 9:2–13

Certain moments change the course of your entire life. When you hear "I do" or "Guilty" or "He didn't make it," you just know that nothing will ever be quite the same. The Transfiguration is one of those moments in Jesus's life. This mountaintop revelation changed everything. No longer could Jesus be viewed simply as a rabbi or as the Messiah. He is God's own Son.

This changed everything for Peter. As an old man, he wrote these words: "When he received honor and glory from God the Father, and the voice was borne to him by the Majestic Glory, 'This is my beloved Son, with whom I am well pleased,' we ourselves heard this very voice borne from heaven, for we were with him on the holy mountain" (2 Peter 1:17–18).

Timing

The story begins six days after Peter's great confession that Jesus was "the Christ, the Son of the living God" (Matthew 16:16). Jesus's disciples finally realized that he was the Messiah. However, almost every Jewish description of the Messiah presented him as a warrior, conquering Israel's enemies with physical violence. But that's the opposite of Jesus. He suffered for his enemies rather than making his enemies suffer. That's why Jesus had to clarify Peter's confession as quickly as it fell from his lips (Mark 8:31).

Only after Jesus laid down his life would God raise him up. "He humbled himself by becoming obedient to the point of death, even death on a cross. Therefore God has highly exalted him and bestowed on him the name that is above every name" (Philippians 2:8–9). The Transfiguration showed a glimpse of Jesus's future.

The six days are a literal reference to Peter's confession. But they also have a deeper, figurative meaning. In the Bible, big things happen after six days. God completed creation in six days (Genesis 2:2). Then he rested—not because he was tired but because his creation would need a weekly reminder of their Creator. That's why he commanded Israel to celebrate Sabbath every week (Exodus 20:8–11).

It was after six days that God spoke to Moses on the mountain: "On the seventh day he called to Moses out of the midst of the cloud. Now the appearance of the glory of the LORD was like a devouring fire on the top of the mountain in the sight of the people of Israel" (Exodus 24:16–17). Six days, you see, are more than just a time frame. They're shouting to the reader, *This is huge!*

The witnesses of this majestic moment were Peter, James, and John—Jesus's inner circle. They would also be with him in the Garden of Gethsemane. Surprisingly, the disciples slept through both of these major events. Perhaps this is a subtle warning to all of us. We can easily sleep through majestic moments.

Transfiguration

The Gospels report that on the mountain Jesus was changed. The Greek word is *metamorphoō*, from which we get *metamorphosis*. This is the right word for such a radical transformation. Jesus's face shone like the sun (Matthew 17:2), and his clothes became dazzling white (Mark 9:3).

The disciples awoke to find Jesus in conversation with Moses and Elijah. Moses was the founder of the nation of Israel. Elijah was her greatest prophet. The two were featured in every account of Hebrew history. They were the greatest miracle workers of the Old Testament, and both were predicted to return someday (Deuteronomy 18:16–18; Malachi 4:5–6).

Is it any surprise that Peter wanted to hang out longer? "Rabbi, it is good that we are here. Let us make three tents, one for you and one for Moses and one for Elijah" (Mark 9:5). Sounds like a good idea, but *God* actually rebuked him: "This is my beloved Son; listen to him" (verse 7).

What God was saying to Peter—and to us—is that no one should be compared to Jesus. As high as Peter's opinion was of Jesus, it wasn't nearly high enough. Peter wanted to put him on level ground with Moses and Elijah—the greatest heroes of the Hebrew faith. However, this moment reveals just how high God holds his own Son. No one can stand in his shadow or be spoken of in the same breath. He is God's Son, the divine sacrifice for the sins of the world.

Exodus

Moses and Elijah disappeared. The voice of God went silent. The disciples had so many questions: *Why must Jesus suffer? Why must Elijah come before the Messiah? Why would Jesus need to rise from the dead?* The answer is one word: *exodus,* which is translated "departure" (Luke 9:31). Jesus fulfilled the entire story of Moses's Exodus. He is the Passover lamb, the shepherd of God's people, the giver of the law, the manna, the rock that provided water in the desert. All this would be fulfilled in Jesus's death and resurrection.

The Transfiguration captures a lot of the Bible in a single event. God spoke from a cloud, which reminds us of the cloud that led the Israelites (Exodus 13:21–22). The cloud also reflects the glory of God's presence (19:16) and foreshadows Jesus's future return (Daniel 7:13; Mark 14:62; 1

Thessalonians 4:17). The voice of God echoes his voice at Jesus's baptism. The six days remind us of creation and the law. The sleepy disciples point forward to Gethsemane. And the talk of the Exodus looks back to Israel in the desert and forward to the Crucifixion. Jesus's transformation gives a glimpse of his resurrection, and the high mountain hints at his ascension. Jesus can't be compared to the greatest heroes of the faith. He can be compared only to God himself. So, is Jesus divine? The Transfiguration shouts, "Yes!"

Key Points

- The Transfiguration is the turning point of Jesus's ministry. From here on, he is God's Son, not just Israel's Messiah.

- Peter thought he was elevating Jesus by comparing him to Moses and Elijah, but he underestimated the honor God gave Jesus.

- The Transfiguration summarizes the major events of the Bible.

This Week

❑ **Day 1 (Eyes):** After reading the essay, answer this question: Have you underestimated Jesus's majesty or divinity?

❑ **Day 2 (Ears):** What predictions in Malachi 3–4 were fulfilled by John the Baptist and Jesus?

❑ **Day 3 (Heart):** Think about who Jesus is based on 2 Corinthians 3:7, Philippians 2:8–11, and 2 Peter 1:16–18.

❑ **Day 4 (Voice):** Discussion:

- What are some of the popular opinions you've heard about Jesus?
- Share about a time when you helped raise someone's understanding or opinion of Jesus. What did you say or do to show who Jesus is?
- Did this passage teach you anything new about Jesus?
- If someone from another religion were to watch you for a week, what would you need to change so she could see that your actions align with what you say you believe about Jesus?

❑ **Day 5 (Hands):** Ask a close friend if he or she can see an area of your life where you're not living up to what you say you believe about Jesus.

18

Does Jesus Care About My Pain?

Biblical Concept: Pain
Read: Mark 1:29–39

My daughter was probably six at the time. My wife and I went to one of those now-extinct stores where you could rent a video. No, not a DVD or Blu-ray. We're talking the "be kind and rewind" type. As we looked for a movie, we lost track of our daughter. When we went to check out, we found her roaming the aisles, policing the videos. Any video with scantily clad women on the cover she flipped backward so the naughtiness was hidden, at least temporarily.

That's a pretty good picture of Jesus's miracles. He didn't offer permanent solutions with physical healings. After all, everyone Jesus healed eventually died. But Jesus did, in the moment, flip the script of Satan. He undid the effect of sin and sickness as a promise of his permanent healing through the Cross. What my daughter did in the video store was just a statement. What Jesus did through his healings was a prophetic promise of full and final healing. Therefore, each miracle is a window into the world to come. Mark 1:29–39 takes us back to the earliest period of Jesus's healing ministry, before the massive crowds or public confrontations. Here we get a glimpse of the pristine Jesus who took the world by storm.

Peter's Mother-in-Law

In the archaeological site of Capernaum, there's a beautiful fifth-century synagogue (Jewish house of worship) built right on top of an earlier synagogue. Chances are good that this is the very spot where Jesus preached in the first century! Close by, a Catholic church stands above a first-century home. Archaeologists found fishhooks and Christian graffiti on the site. Many (or perhaps most) suggest that Peter likely lived in this very house with his wife and mother-in-law, as well as his brother, Andrew. This makes sense since it's just a few yards from the lake where he made his living.

We can picture Jesus worshipping in the synagogue, reading from the Torah scroll, and praying the Shema (Deuteronomy 6:4–9). After the final "Amen," they strolled back to the house, a two-minute walk. Peter's mother-in-law was bedridden with a fever. The Greek word is a form of the word for "fire." In other words, she was in trouble; you might say "a hot mess." Her symptoms may indicate malaria. Today malaria is treatable. Back then it was often deadly.

Luke said Jesus "rebuked the fever" (4:39). That's interesting because Jesus also rebuked demons, ordering them away (verses 35, 41). He treated this sickness like any other satanic attack. Jesus took Peter's mother-in-law by the hand and lifted her from her sickbed. She immediately began to serve as hostess. Not only was she healed of the fever. She was *completely* restored!

Word Gets Out

"That evening at sundown they brought to him all who were sick or oppressed by demons" (Mark 1:32). The news of Jesus's healing power spread. Everyone from miles around showed up at Peter's humble home. People carried cots, hobbled on crutches, ran with children in their arms. The bruised, fatigued, and bandaged pushed for time with Jesus. It was a pit of human pain, and Jesus waded into the middle of it.

This took most of the night. But Mark simply stated, "He healed many who were sick with various diseases, and cast out many demons" (verse 34). We can imagine the scene. Jesus took his time with each individual as if he were the only one there. "How long have you had this? Who brought you here? You know, God loves you, and you are immensely important to him." Each interview was intimate. Each encounter was personal. Each healing created a new wave of celebration, undoing the work of the Evil One. This is the image of what Eden could look like again.

Jesus knew they would all fall prey again to Satan's rude awakening. Yet for this moment, at this place, a small part of the kingdom broke through. It was the beginning of the end of Satan's reign. This world was about to be overtaken by love.

He Took Our Infirmities

Matthew, as he so often did, quoted an Old Testament passage: "This was to fulfill what was spoken by the prophet Isaiah: 'He took our illnesses and bore our diseases'" (8:17). The citation is from Isaiah 53:4. Wait a minute. Isn't that passage talking about our spiritual condition? Which is it? Healing of our bodies or healing of our souls? The answer is . . . yes.

The healing of our bodies is a temporary gift of God. Not everyone receives physical healing, and everyone who receives it eventually dies. Our ultimate healing is the restoration of our souls. That's the power of the gospel. While the curse of sin will eventually get the best of our bodies, the salvation of our souls will lead to new bodies, a new Jerusalem, a restoration of Eden. Then we will stand together as they did in the streets of Capernaum that night.

Where Is Jesus When You Need Him?

After the very long evening, the apostles crashed. Rightly so. Early the next morning, the crowds came knocking again. Jesus, however, was nowhere to be found. The search party was put on alert. When Peter finally found him, with a tone of frustration he said, "Everyone is looking for you" (Mark 1:37), as if he thought Jesus had FOMO.

Unfazed, Jesus simply responded to Peter, "Let us go on to the next towns, that I may preach there also, for that is why I came out" (verse 38). And that they did, throughout all Galilee, from town to town and synagogue to synagogue.

Jesus showed us that there's no time to be complacent. There are more hurting people to help, more territories to take, more videos to flip over. Does Jesus care about your pain? Yes. *Yes.* And he cares about the pain of others that you may be able to alleviate. Let's join him in reducing pain wherever it's found.

Key Points

- Jesus's miracles were momentary relief, pointing to his ultimate agenda of salvation of body, soul, and spirit.

- Jesus is concerned about the whole person. He desires healing in every area of your life, though your spirit is the priority, for it will result in the healing of your body and soul in eternity.

- We can't be satisfied with momentary gains like Capernaum. There's still more territory to be taken over from Satan.

This Week

❑ **Day 1 (Eyes):** After reading the essay, answer this question: Is your greatest need right now physical, emotional, or spiritual? How are these three related?

❑ **Day 2 (Ears):** According to Leviticus 26:1–26, how does (dis)obedience to God's commands relate to disease and disasters?

❑ **Day 3 (Heart):** Think about Hebrews 12:12–13, James 5:16, and 1 Peter 2:24. How are physical and spiritual healing connected?

❑ **Day 4 (Voice):** Discussion:
- Have you ever known or heard about someone who was healed miraculously?
- Why do you think people often prioritize their physical health over their spiritual health?
- Why do you think people who are sick are often more open to spiritual conversations?
- Is there anything you've been thinking about doing to care for people's physical needs that could open opportunities to share Christ's love for them? What would you need to take your next step toward that goal?

❑ **Day 5 (Hands):** Do one thing this week to alleviate physical suffering for someone.

19

Can Jesus Make Me Clean?

Biblical Concept: Purity
Read: Mark 1:40–45

Billy was the most irritating student I ever had. One day I didn't see him in class. I'll admit that I was relieved as I called roll. He responded from *underneath my desk.* Remember, I taught college, not middle school! I rebuked him sternly. Then the Holy Spirit rebuked me: *You don't even know him. Take him to lunch. Learn his story.* At lunch Billy captivated me with the story of his life. It was tragic.

Had I been through half as much as Billy, I wouldn't be half the man he is. In that moment, I realized that *people who are unlovely are unlovely not because they're unlovable but because they're unloved.* This truth is at the heart of this leper's story.

Yuck!

Today leprosy is labeled as Hansen's disease. It's a bacterial infection affecting the nervous system. Because it deadens the nerves, damage to the skin and muscles can go undetected and untreated. This often results in disfigurement, crippling of hands and feet, and even blindness. With modern medicine, Hansen's disease is treatable. In biblical times, your only hope was an intervention from God himself.

Leviticus 13 describes leprosy as extremely contagious and dangerous. Not to mention just gross! A person with leprosy could have a swelling, a scab, or a bright spot (verse 2). The hair on the sore spot turned white (verse 3). Sometimes the disease left raw flesh (verse 14); at other times it resulted in a boil (verses 18–20). Hair could turn yellow or thin out (verse 30). Infected spots might have had reddish-white sores (verses 42–43). Worst of all, it was so contagious that it could pass from person to person on surfaces as diverse as leather and plaster walls (verses 48–49; 14:37–41).

Several notable people in the Old Testament got leprosy: Miriam (Numbers 12:9–14), Naaman (2 Kings 5:1–27), and Uzziah (2 Chronicles 26:17–23). In the New Testament, a group of ten lepers were healed by Jesus (Luke 17:12–19), not to mention the unnamed leper in this story, who was the first person to ask Jesus to heal him. He saw something divine in Jesus.

The Direction of Contagion

According to Leviticus 13:45, "The leprous person who has the disease shall wear torn clothes and let the hair of his head hang loose, and he shall cover his upper lip and cry out, 'Unclean, unclean.'" This was to keep lepers in quarantine. One famous rabbi, Johanan, said it was forbidden to walk within six feet of a leper (the same social distancing requirement as for COVID-19). But if the wind was blowing toward you, another rabbi said 150 feet wouldn't be enough. Rabbi Lakish boasted that he pelted lepers with rocks to keep them away.[1] This was serious social distancing. Adding insult to injury, leprosy had the reputation of being a curse from God for sin.

It's a fair guess that when this leper approached Jesus, most in the crowd took a step back and gasped. They knew the leper was contagious. They believed he was sinful. So when Jesus reached out to touch him, it must have been a slow-motion moment with Peter recoiling and yelling, "Noooooo!"

"Immediately the leprosy left him, and he was made clean" (Mark 1:42). This short statement is a fraction of a tweet. Yet it would change religion forever, setting Christianity apart from every other faith. Religious people have always practiced "spiritual distancing." Other religions have sacred spaces where sinners aren't allowed. They practice rituals of purification and have moral laws that keep them separate—don't drink; don't intermarry; don't socialize with sinners.

With one touch, Jesus rewrote the laws of spiritual physics: *cleanness is more contagious than uncleanness.* Rather than going on a social media rant, he simply touched the outcast. The crowd gasped. But then they saw with their own eyes that Jesus's cleanness had passed to the leper. His skin was restored, and their view of religious purity was turned on its head.

Cure Versus Healing

There's a difference between a healing and a cure. A cure deals with the physical crisis. A healing, however, goes further. Most diseases come with more problems than just the physical sickness. For example, the COVID-19 quarantine caused a rise in depression. Why? Because sickness separates us from those we love, a pain that can be far greater than the physical suffering.

Jesus did two things to move this from a cure to a healing. First, he touched the leper. That was undoubtedly the leper's first human contact since his diagnosis. Sometimes a hand on a shoulder or a hug can do more for healing than the strongest medications.

Second, Jesus said, "Go, show yourself to the priest and offer for your cleansing what Moses commanded, for a proof to them" (verse 44). Here's why. Jesus knew that once he passed the test of the priest, he could finally be reconciled to his community.

Just in case you're wondering, Jesus hasn't changed. You may pray for a cure. Jesus will never be satisfied with that. He wants you to be healed—

fully restored to the people you love. Furthermore, he calls us to follow his lead, welcoming those the world tends to keep at a distance. What would Jesus do if he were you? Go do that.

Key Points

- Leprosy was a terrible disease. It was contagious and disfiguring, but it also made people think you were a sinner cursed by God.

- Jesus proved that cleanness is more contagious than uncleanness.

- Jesus isn't satisfied with a cure for your body; he wants to restore your relationships.

This Week

☐ **Day 1 (Eyes):** After reading the essay, think about your prayers. Are you asking for enough? Do you want a cure or a healing?

☐ **Day 2 (Ears):** Read the story of Naaman the leper, who was cleansed in 2 Kings 5. What lessons can you learn about your own faith and prayer life?

☐ **Day 3 (Heart):** Think about 2 Corinthians 7:1, Ephesians 5:26, and 2 Timothy 2:21. According to these verses, what does it mean to be clean?

☐ **Day 4 (Voice):** Discussion:
- What kinds of people are avoided because they are "unclean"?
- Who of the people you know is good at including individuals who others might avoid?
- Do you believe that cleanness is more contagious than uncleanness? Can you provide an example?
- Is there a person you deliberately avoid that you could have a positive impact on?

☐ **Day 5 (Hands):** Go to one person you typically avoid, and ask this question: "Would you be willing to tell me your story?" If she asks for clarification, simply say you want to hear a bit about her life so you can understand her better.

20

Is Jesus Impressed with Me?

Biblical Concept: Inclusion
Read: Luke 7:1–10

Caleb came into my classroom like a whirlwind. He was clearly clever and very entertaining but weird. By *weird,* I mean awkward. I didn't know what to do with him. I liked him, but he was high mainte-nance. Only later would I learn that both his parents were gay and his mother engaged in witchcraft. For someone planning to be in ministry, he had a lot stacked against him.

However, by sheer tenacity and willpower, he has become a sought-after speaker, a bestselling author, a church consultant, and the single most connected person I know. In short, he's very impressive! How does that happen? Well, we're about to find out.

The Background of the Centurion

In Jesus's day, Israel was an occupied state. Rome built entire cities as outposts in Israel. These places introduced cultural practices forbidden to faithful Jews. So when one of the lieutenants in the Roman army was stationed in Capernaum, a heavily Jewish area, that was riot worthy. Surprisingly, this particular lieutenant—what they called a centurion—was loved by the locals.

Centurion (literally a leader of one hundred men) was the highest rank an enlisted man could hope to achieve. Roman officers came only from elite families. That made centurions the most important link between the troops and the officers. They understood both worlds and were therefore essential to the military machine.

This centurion of Capernaum is mentioned alongside four other centurions in the New Testament: the centurion at Jesus's crucifixion, who proclaimed him to be "the Son of God" (Matthew 27:54); Cornelius, the first Gentile convert to Christianity (Acts 10); the centurion who stopped Paul's beating when he learned Paul was a Roman citizen (Acts 22:25–26); and Julius, who accompanied Paul to Rome, showing him honor and kindness (Acts 27). All of them are portrayed in a positive light. Think about that. They were lieutenants in the occupying enemy forces yet still respected by those whose land they were invading. They won over the locals by serving the community.

For example, this centurion built the synagogue in Capernaum, likely employing his own troops in the construction. Soldiers also helped build Romans roads, some of which are still standing today as footpaths near archaeological sites. By providing labor, they would gain favor with the community, especially those devout Jews who were most likely to stir up a riot.

It's also possible this centurion was a convert to Judaism—kind of. Many Romans were attracted to the one God of Judaism and the ethics of Scripture, which were lacking in their own religion. If the centurion accepted the faith but refused to get circumcised, he would become what they called a God-fearer. He was still an outsider, but his financial contributions put him right next to the inner circle.

The Request of the Centurion

This centurion in Capernaum had a servant who fell ill. He wasn't just any servant. He was like a son to him (Matthew 8:6). This was fairly common. Many servants were actually adopted into the family. This poor lad was at death's door, and the centurion was at his wit's end, distraught over his potential loss.

When he heard about Jesus and his ability to heal, he called in a favor. He asked the Jewish elders to approach Jesus on his behalf and request a favor for their friend. "They pleaded with [Jesus] earnestly, saying, 'He is worthy to have you do this for him, for he loves our nation, and he is the one who built us our synagogue'" (Luke 7:4–5). Jesus agreed to go with them.

While Jesus was on his way, a second delegation was sent. The centurion's messengers asked Jesus *not* to enter his house. Why? The centurion knew that by crossing his threshold, Jesus would become unclean in the eyes of the local Jews. He said, "Lord, do not trouble yourself, for I am not worthy to have you come under my roof. Therefore I did not presume to come to you" (verses 6–7). It was actually a very thoughtful gesture.

The Faith of the Centurion

The centurion understood Jesus's culture. He also believed in Jesus's ability. Several months earlier, Jesus healed an official's son in Capernaum. The catch was that Jesus healed the boy from Cana, fourteen miles away (John 4:46–54). We can assume the centurion was familiar with the healing and this gave him hope that Jesus not only could heal but could also command the healing from a distance.

As a military man, he understood the chain of command. The emperor in Rome would give a command, and the generals carried it out on the battlefield far away. The centurion assumed that this sickness was part of the unseen army of spiritual forces. He believed that Jesus had the authority to give orders to angels and demons. In his own words to Jesus, "Say the word, and let my servant be healed" (Luke 7:7).

His faith was so amazing that it amazed even Jesus. Think about that. What must it take to amaze Jesus? He turned to the crowd that followed him and said, "I tell you, not even in Israel have I found such faith" (verse 9).

Only two times was Jesus amazed. Here with the centurion and in Nazareth, his hometown (Mark 6:6). But there he was amazed by his neighbors' *lack* of faith. Those who knew Jesus best had little faith. This centurion, who never actually met Jesus face to face, had faith greater than any Israelite. That's impressive.

This brings us back to our initial question: Is Jesus impressed with you? If the answer is yes, it has little to do with your background, morality, or even religious devotion. It has everything to do with your belief in him. Such faith will be demonstrated by trust and loyalty.

Key Points

- Centurions in the New Testament are painted in a good light. This shows the paradox that outsiders are often more full of faith than insiders.

- The centurion amazed Jesus by his faith, which is impressive since the only other time Jesus was amazed was by his own hometown's *lack* of faith.

- If you impress Jesus, it will be by your faith in him.

This Week

❏ **Day 1 (Eyes):** After reading the essay, do you think Jesus is impressed with you?

❏ **Day 2 (Ears):** Abraham is known as the father of faith. Read his story in Genesis 12:1–9 and 14:1–24. What similarities does this centurion have with Abraham?

❏ **Day 3 (Heart):** Think about Acts 10:1–8, 22–23, 28–29, and 34–35. How does the story of Cornelius reflect Jesus's encounter with the centurion?

❏ **Day 4 (Voice):** Discussion:
- Share a story of someone who surprised you in a positive way.
- What does Hebrews 11:1 mean?
- Why do you think outsiders are often clearer about who Jesus is than insiders?
- If you're willing to be vulnerable, what is an area of your life that you really haven't trusted Jesus with?

❏ **Day 5 (Hands):** Approach someone you think is far from God, and ask this question: "Hey, I was just curious—what do you believe about Jesus?"

21

Can Jesus Restore My Relationships?

Biblical Concept: Restoration
Read: Mark 5:21–43

Bob was an older mentor and a dear friend. But then I did something unintentionally that deeply hurt him. When I discovered how I had hurt him, I tried to apologize. Unfortunately, it was too deep and too late. We lost contact. Several years later, Bob died. This is one of my greatest regrets. Broken relationships are painful. That's why Jesus's healings are designed not only to cure our ills but also to restore our relationships. This story shows Jesus's desire for relational restoration.

A Twelve-Year-Old at Death's Door

Jesus arrived in Capernaum after a loooooooong night! He and the boys were nearly capsized by a storm in the middle of the lake. Jesus ordered the storm into submission. Spooky! Once ashore, they were confronted by a raging demoniac. Jesus subdued the demons as easily as he had the storm. He cast them into some pigs; the pigs rushed into the lake and drowned. The villagers freaked out and asked Jesus to leave. He did. Now he was back home in Capernaum.

As soon as he stepped ashore, he was mobbed. The first to break through was Jairus, a ruler of the synagogue. His only child, a daughter, was knocking at death's door.

What father wouldn't ask for healing for his little girl? She was twelve years old, which was when girls became women in Israel. At this point, it wasn't likely that Jairus and his wife were able to have any more children. Jairus fell at Jesus's feet. This kneeling was the same devotion shown by the demoniac the night before and the woman who was about to stop Jesus in his tracks.

A Bloody Interruption

As Jesus made his way to Jairus's home, the mob "thronged" him (Mark 5:24). This word means "to press hard, like a vise." It indicates the potential danger of the crowd. Somehow a woman made her way to Jesus. She'd been bleeding for twelve years. This was, most likely, a gynecological problem. Mark noted that she "had suffered much under many physicians, and had spent all that she had, and was no better but rather grew worse" (verse 26). We can assume a number of things about her life: (1) Since they lacked disposable sanitary products in those days, the whole village knew about her problem. They saw her going to the lake daily to wash out her undergarments, bedsheets, and clothes. (2) She was thin and weak. (3) A foul odor followed her everywhere she went. (4) She was considered unclean under Jewish law (Leviticus 15:25–33).

She knew Jesus might be her only hope. She mustered all the energy she had left and muscled through the crowd. Coming up behind Jesus, she grabbed ahold of "the fringe of his garment" (Matthew 9:20). She believed that if she could touch the tassels of Jesus's prayer shawl, she could "steal" some of his healing power.

It worked! "Immediately the flow of blood dried up, and she felt in her body that she was healed of her disease" (Mark 5:29). Jesus stopped in his tracks. "Who touched my garments?" he asked (verse 30). Well, lots of people; he was in a crowd! However, he knew that someone had touched him with faith and that God had honored that person's effort with healing. He turned. It was no secret. There she was, trembling at his feet.

Why would Jesus out her like that? Because he knew that she needed not only a cure for her physical problem but also a restoration of her relationships. Without a public declaration of cleansing, how could she be restored to her husband's arms, her circle of friends, her worship in the synagogue? Jesus affirmed her faith: "Daughter, your faith has made you well; go in peace" (verse 34). This word *peace* is equivalent to the Hebrew *shalom*. Jesus was setting her world right. And she was the only person Jesus ever called "daughter." How he loved her!

From Death to Life

Jairus's servants interrupted the procession. The news was jarring: "Your daughter is dead" (verse 35). They weren't pulling any punches. However, I can imagine Jesus putting both hands on Jairus's shoulders and saying, "Do not fear, only believe" (verse 36).

They arrived at the house, and Jesus stunned the crowd by saying, "Why are you making a commotion and weeping? The child is not dead but sleeping" (verse 39). The crowd flipped from mourning to mocking. They might be ancients, but they weren't ignorant. They knew when a person was dead.

Taking only Peter, James, and John, Jesus entered the house. With the parents watching, Jesus took the girl by the hand and said to her in Aramaic, "*Talitha cumi*," meaning, "Little girl, I say to you, arise" (verse 41). The girl immediately got up and started walking.

What Do These Two Women Mean?

The little girl was twelve years old; the older woman had been bleeding for twelve years. Biblical numbers often have symbolic meaning. Three represents God; four represents humans. And 3 x 4 = 12. These two women represent God doing something *extraordinary* among humans.

The woman's problem was blood. The girl's problem was death. Question: Where else in the Gospels are blood and death mentioned in the same story? That's right—the cross of Christ. These paired healings point us to the Cross. It offers forgiveness, but that's not all. The cross of Christ restores us to our heavenly Father *and* typically brings restoration to many of our earthly relationships. These two women offer a promise of what Jesus can do for us.

Key Points

- The bleeding woman and the dead girl had not just a physical problem but also a social problem—separation from those they cared about most.

- Twelve years tie the two women together, so we read their stories in tandem, knowing they represent God doing something extraordinary in our midst.

- Blood and death point forward to the cross of Christ, which restores our relationship with God and often with others as well.

This Week

❏ **Day I (Eyes):** After reading the essay, answer this question: Do you have a relationship that needs to be restored?

❏ **Day 2 (Ears):** Read the story of Ruth. How does she represent redemption and restoration?

❏ **Day 3 (Heart):** Think about Luke 8:2–3, Philippians 4:2–3, and James 2:25. What do these verses tell us about women, redemption, and restoration in Christianity?

❏ **Day 4 (Voice):** Discussion:
- What advice would you give to help two friends reconcile after a conflict?
- When there's tension in relationships, do you tend to jump in as a peacemaker, or do you tend to back away?
- What do you observe Jesus doing with this woman and with Jairus's daughter that you might use to help restore relationships in your circle of influence?
- Do you have any relationships you would like Jesus to restore?

❏ **Day 5 (Hands):** If you're experiencing any relational separation, offer that person either forgiveness or an apology or both. Share with him that this is prompted by the realization of what Jesus has done for you.

22

Can Jesus Give Me Life?

Biblical Concept: Life
Read: John 11:17–44

Funerals can be awkward. We dress in black but decorate the church with bright flowers. We say the nicest things about the deceased, even if some of it is a little exaggerated. Afterward, we eat a potluck meal. Strange.

Death itself is unnatural. We sense that we were made for eternity. God never intended us to die. But alas, there was sin. Perhaps that's what we're feeling at funerals: human responsibility in the downward spiral of God's good creation. Jesus felt it too. Let's watch his reaction at one of his best friends' funeral.

The Setting

John recorded seven signs. As we've seen, they aren't just miracles of power. They point to Jesus's ultimate purpose in our lives. Each of the seven signs represents an important step in discipleship. Raising Lazarus from the dead is the seventh and greatest sign. As such, this event is the epicenter of John's gospel.

This story takes place in Bethany, a village two miles east of Jerusalem. It was the home of Lazarus and his two sisters, Mary and Martha, who had sent a delegation to Jesus with an emergency message. Lazarus was at death's door. They asked Jesus to come quickly. The Master sent back this message: "This illness does not lead to death. It is for the glory of God, so that the Son of God may be glorified through it" (John 11:4). Sounds optimistic. However, Lazarus died while the messengers were with Jesus. Jesus wouldn't show up for four more days. Jews believed that the spirit could linger around the corpse for up to three days. Day four meant even the ghost was gone. Jesus's optimism seems misplaced.

Jesus Ministered to Martha

Martha greeted Jesus first. Her words, intended as praise, contained a veiled complaint: "If you had been here, my brother would not have died" (verse 21). She still believed, however, that Jesus could do *something:* "Even now I know that whatever you ask from God, God will give you" (verse 22).

Jesus, trying to raise her level of faith, replied, "Your brother will rise again" (verse 23). Martha responded, "I know that he will rise again in the resurrection on the last day" (verse 24). She still didn't get it. Jesus said, "I am the resurrection and the life" (verse 25; see John 6:39–40, 44, 54; 1 Corinthians 6:14; 15:20–28; 2 Corinthians 4:14). He was claiming, "I am here right now, the author of life." Jesus asked her, "Do you believe this?" (John 11:26). She dutifully replied, "Yes, Lord; I believe that you are the Christ, the Son of God" (verse 27). It's beautiful but empty. She was doing what most of us do in crisis. We say the right thing, then walk away, missing what Jesus has offered!

Jesus Ministered to Mary

As soon as Mary saw Jesus, she fell at his feet. In fact, every time Mary is mentioned, she's at Jesus's feet (Luke 10:39; John 12:3). She said to Jesus the exact same words her sister had: "If you had been here, my brother would not have died" (John 11:32).

Although their words were identical, Jesus's response to these two women couldn't have been more different. Martha's statement moved Jesus to a theological discussion. Mary's emotions moved him to tears. At Mary's pain, Jesus was deeply troubled. The Greek word for "troubled" is used for churning water. Without a doubt, this moment affected Jesus.

What was it that troubled Jesus? The sadness of his friends? Death itself? Perhaps it was their lack of faith or his own impending death. It was probably a combination of all these. This much we know: Jesus doesn't sit idly on the sidelines. He feels your pain because he has walked your path. He will sit with you and whisper, "I know." He does.

Standing in front of the stone, knowing what he was about to do, Jesus did the most amazing thing. He wept. John 11:35 is the shortest verse in the English Bible, yet few are filled with as much meaning. The moment wasn't lost on the crowd. They said, "See how he loved him!" (verse 36). He loves you too.

Jesus Ministered to Lazarus

After the stone was rolled away, Jesus lifted up his eyes and prayed. Notice in verse 42, in the prayer, he admitted that this petition was for the sake of the crowd standing there, not for him or his Father. Then he cried, "Lazarus, come out" (verse 43). *And Lazarus did!* Since Lazarus was wrapped from head to toe, the only way of escape was to hop up the stairs from the tomb. That must have been a frightful sight. Jesus had to remind them, "Unbind him, and let him go" (verse 44). This would be hilarious if it weren't for this deadly serious observation: Lazarus represents *us*.

What Jesus did for Lazarus predicted Jesus's own resurrection. It promises our future resurrection. *And* it depicts the life Jesus wants to give us *now*. He has called your name; death has been conquered—so take off the graveclothes and come out to experience life. As Jesus asked Martha, "Do you believe this?" Like Martha, we say we believe but still underestimate Jesus. He has promised life, full and free. Not in the future. *Now!*

Key Points

- Martha and Mary both approached Jesus with the same statement yet got totally different responses. Jesus will meet you where you are and with what you need.

- Jesus knew he was going to raise Lazarus yet was swept up in the emotions of the moment. He feels what you feel and will stand with you in your grief.

- The raising of Lazarus is a sign not only of what Jesus will do for us but also of what he has already done for us spiritually.

This Week

❏ **Day 1 (Eyes):** After reading the essay, what area of your life would you like Jesus to breathe life into?

❏ **Day 2 (Ears):** Read 1 Kings 17:8–24 and 2 Kings 4:18–37. What similarities are there between Jesus raising Lazarus, and Elijah and Elisha raising someone from the dead?

❏ **Day 3 (Heart):** Think about 1 Corinthians 6:14, 1 Corinthians 15:20–28, and 2 Corinthians 4:14. How do these promises that Jesus will raise us from the dead compare to what he did for Lazarus?

❏ **Day 4 (Voice):** Discussion:

- Have you had someone close to you die? What was that experience like?
- Do you think most people are afraid to die? How can you tell?
- Why does death feel so unnatural to us? What could you do to live without that fear of death?
- What area of your life right now could use a bit more life? How could Jesus speak life into that area?

❏ **Day 5 (Hands):** This may seem a bit awkward, but it could give you important insight. Sit down and write your own obituary. What do you want people to remember about how you lived?

23

Can Jesus Forgive Me?

Biblical Concept: Forgiveness
Read: Mark 2:1–17

Jason is the kind of guy that others envy in the gym. Plus, his business is booming, and he has connections all over the world. But he also has a past. Though it made him the man he is today, it took him a while to get past his past. He struggled with accepting the forgiveness Jesus offered. Once, while Jason was wrestling with his personal history, I sat down next to him and said, "God wants you to *know* that you are forgiven." It's difficult to describe the power of that moment. It was as if he got his legs spiritually. He didn't just walk; he hit a dead run!

How to Break into an Ancient Home

The house was packed. The single entrance into the courtyard was blocked. There was no more standing room, and no one else was getting in.

This was unacceptable to four friends. Their buddy had been paralyzed and needed healing. They carried him on a pallet to the place Jesus was preaching, but there was no way in, and no one was moving. Being resourceful fellows, they carried the paralytic to the roof. That's a bit scary, especially if you're the one lying paralyzed! Jesus was standing under an awning. He knew something was up by the crowd's distraction but couldn't see what these guys were up to.

They dropped down to the awning with a thud and started digging. These courtyard coverings were typically thatch—branches woven together and covered with grass and mud. Often they were built in sections. So, once they dug through the edges of the section, it would be easy enough to remove. In the meantime, Jesus would be pelted with debris while trying to make the next point in his message. Suddenly the sunlight broke through. The four friends lowered the paralytic right in front of Jesus, then peeked over the edge to watch.

The Healing We Need Most

The friends wanted their buddy to walk. The paralytic would rather work for a living than beg for money. It was a legitimate need but not his ultimate need.

Seeing their faith, Jesus said, "Son, your sins are forgiven" (Mark 2:5). Notice, it was the *friends'* faith that moved Jesus. Don't miss this. Our faith in what Jesus can do for others can move him to action. They must have been both confused and delighted. In their culture, they would have assumed that sin caused his paralysis. So to declare his sins forgiven would also have been a promise of healing. But why didn't Jesus just heal the guy and get back to his sermon? Well, because his healing would be the more important message, not just for the four friends but also for the skeptical scribes.

The scribes in the crowd were professional copyists of the Old Testament Scriptures. Their occupation made them legal experts and watchdogs for false teaching. They thought they'd found some. "Who can forgive sins but God alone?" (verse 7). They were outraged.

Jesus knew what they were thinking. "Which is easier, to say to the paralytic, 'Your sins are forgiven,' or to say, 'Rise, take up your bed and walk'?" (verse 9). Well, both are easy to *say*. That's the point! Anyone can say, "Your sins are forgiven," but it matters only when the divine Judge declares it so. Likewise, anyone can tell a paralytic to walk, but to pull it off, you must have God's power.

Jesus had that divine authority. He said, "Rise, pick up your bed, and go home" (verse 11). The paralytic did. The argument instantly ended, giving way to public praise. "They were all amazed and glorified God, saying, 'We never saw anything like this!'" (verse 12).

Matthew and the New Movement

Jesus went straight from the house to the lake, where a man named Matthew (also known as Levi) was collecting money from the local fishermen. Matthew's title, *mokhes* (tax collector), is related to the word for "oppression."[1] He was despised.

Jesus called Matthew: "Follow me" (verse 14). Peter was thinking, *No . . . not him!* A despised tax collector couldn't possibly help the movement. Then Matthew did the unthinkable. He left his tax-collection booth and followed Jesus. This is incredible! Peter and John could always go back to fishing if this Jesus thing didn't pan out (and after the Resurrection, they did!). Matthew, on the other hand, had a line of sharks behind him, eager to take his spot. Once he walked away, there was no going back.

Matthew was the least likely candidate to become an apostle. Nonetheless, of all the gospel writers, he quoted the most Old Testament scripture. His alliance with a secular government made him look uninterested in the Jesus movement. But he was longing and searching for something more than money could buy. When Jesus offered him the opportunity, he dove in headfirst.

Then Matthew threw a party and invited all his sketchy friends. This made the religious leaders and the other disciples quite uncomfortable. But Jesus intervened: "Those who are well have no need of a physician, but those who are sick. I came not to call the righteous, but sinners" (verse 17).

This reminds me of my friend Jason. Several years ago, no one would have guessed he would be a serious Jesus follower. Today I know no one else who uses his occupation, connections, and experience to introduce more people to Jesus. Like Matthew, he's a party waiting to happen, but his parties have a purpose—to make Jesus famous. Like the paralytic, it was his friendships that put him in a position to receive Christ's forgiveness.

Here's the bottom line for you and for me: Don't assume that people far from the church are far from faith. They may be the most open to Jesus *and* his most effective ambassadors. Your friendship and faith may be what they need to come to Jesus.

Key Points

- Forgiveness of sins is deeper and more important than physical healing.

- All of us can be forgiven through Jesus Christ if we have faith.

- The paralytic shows the power of friendship to lead to forgiveness, and Matthew reminds us that those you never suspect may be most open to forgiveness.

This Week

☐ **Day 1 (Eyes):** After reading the essay, do you believe your sins have been forgiven fully and forever?

☐ **Day 2 (Ears):** Read Psalm 32. Who of the people you know needs to hear this poem?

☐ **Day 3 (Heart):** According to Romans 4:7, Ephesians 1:7, and Hebrews 9:22, how much confidence can we have that we are forgiven?

☐ **Day 4 (Voice):** Discussion:

- What happens to a person physically, emotionally, and/or spiritually when she isn't forgiven?
- Have you ever felt unforgiven either by God or by another person? What was that like?
- Who in your circle is most like Matthew—a person living without Jesus who you suspect may have interest in Christianity?
- What drew you to faith? Was it a person, an event, or an experience?

☐ **Day 5 (Hands):** Share the story of Matthew with a pre-Christian friend, and ask, "Do you think people assume you're less interested in God than you actually are?"

24

What Do We Need from Jesus?

Biblical Concept: Loyalty
Read: John 5:1–18

A mentor once criticized me, saying that I prioritize people I think I can get something from! It was unkind but only partially untrue, which made it more painful to hear. It caused me to carefully evaluate my friendships and loyalties. I have a problem I'm trying to correct. This story explains why it's such a significant problem.

The Significance of Signs

As we've already seen, signs in the book of John are significant. They are not about Jesus's raw power but about his agenda. Over and over, we see that what people really need is not a miracle from Jesus but Jesus himself. Jesus wants us to come to *him* by faith. The prize is Jesus himself, not some temporary healing or other miracle. This is most clearly seen in the third sign, the healing of a lame man at the Pool of Bethesda.

There's a lot of similarity between this healing and the healing in the previous chapter. Both were paralytics. Both were told, "Get up, take up your bed, and walk" (John 5:8; see Mark 2:11). Both times Jesus was accused of blasphemy, and both times the healing proved Jesus's true identity. The difference? This lame man lacked the faith of a true follower of Jesus.

Sitting by the Pool

Near the Temple Mount in Jerusalem, there's a pool where the locals came for water. It was called Bethesda, which means "house of mercy." According to a local legend, whenever the spring bubbled up, the first one in the pool got healed. That's probably true; after all, the first one in the pool was likely the least sick. The cool, refreshing water, along with a rush of adrenaline, might have accounted for the apparent healing. However, that's hardly how God operates. Over and over, the Scriptures show how God helps the helpless.

One of the most helpless that day was a lame thirty-eight-year-old. This may sound harsh, but I don't like him. And if I explain this clearly, neither will you. He was just one in a crowd of many sick people labeled as "blind, lame, and paralyzed" (John 5:3). Even worse, their sickness was believed to be a curse for some sin. Hence, all these people were considered "bad people."

This lame man had waited a long time for healing. Jesus was prepared to give it: "Do you want to be healed?" (verse 6). Simple question. Obvious answer. But listen to the man's lame answer: "Sir, I have no one to put me into the pool when the water is stirred up, and while I am going another steps down before me" (verse 7). What a whiner! No wonder he had no friends to help him into the pool. He was one of those people who aren't happy unless they have something to complain about.

If I were Jesus (and we're all glad I'm not), I would have said, "Fine. Have it your way," and walked away. Clearly, this healing didn't happen because he deserved it, had faith for it, or requested it. Jesus was making a point, and we'd better not miss it. He said, "Get up, take up your bed, and walk" (verse 8). As soon as Jesus said this, the man was healed and did as Jesus ordered. Good news, right? Not so fast!

Trouble A-Brewin'

As the man walked home, the Jewish leaders stopped him abruptly: "It is the Sabbath, and it is not lawful for you to take up your bed" (verse 10). His heart had to be pounding out of his chest. He was used to the religious elite looking down on him, not confronting him face to face. I do kind of feel sorry for him at this point.

Even so, what he said next is inexcusable: "The man who healed me, that man said to me, 'Take up your bed, and walk'" (verse 11). He flat-out threw Jesus under the bus! They asked him, "Who is the man?" (verse 12). You may not believe this, but the man had no idea who Jesus was! How is that even possible? How can you be healed from a lifelong sickness and *not* find out who changed your life? He didn't know where to send the thank-you note; he didn't even know Jesus's name! Shameful.

Later, Jesus ran across this ex-lame man in the temple: "See, you are well! Sin no more, that nothing worse may happen to you" (verse 14). What in the world? How was this man sinning? He surely wasn't stealing or committing adultery. Jaywalking, perhaps? His sin was simply this: rejecting Jesus. It may not seem like much, but there's nothing that will cost you more dearly in the end. Jesus gave him fair warning.

What did he do? This is tragic and infuriating: "The man went away and told the Jews that it was Jesus who had healed him" (verse 15). He actually took the initiative to tell the rulers the identity and whereabouts of Jesus. Why would he do that? I can think of only one reason—he valued praise from people more than loyalty to Jesus.

Verse 18 spells out the consequences: "This was why the Jews were seeking all the more to kill him, because not only was he breaking the Sabbath, but he was even calling God his own Father, making himself equal with God."

That's precisely what Jesus was doing—claiming to be the Son of God. If he really is, that changes everything, especially what he expects from us. We don't come to him as a genie who can meet our needs. Rather, he expects us to come to him for him. He is the pearl of great price, the grand prize, the Son of the living God.

Key Points

- Typically, the healing of lame men in the New Testament shows what happens spiritually when we demonstrate loyalty to Jesus. In John 5, the lame man is a warning about what happens when we lack loyalty.

- If we are healed physically but not spiritually, we wind up in a worse state.

- Our loyalty to Jesus is driven by who he is, not by what we can gain from him.

This Week

❏ **Day 1 (Eyes):** After reading the essay, do you think you've ever taken Jesus for granted?

❏ **Day 2 (Ears):** Read 1 Samuel 18:1–4; 19:1–7; and 20:1–42. How did Jonathan demonstrate loyalty to David?

❏ **Day 3 (Heart):** Read Romans 4:5, Colossians 1:23, and 1 Thessalonians 1:3, replacing the word *faith* with *loyalty*. Read the verses again, using the word *allegiance*. Did this help you understand these verses differently?

❏ **Day 4 (Voice):** Discussion:

- Have you ever been used by someone? How did that make you feel?
- What comes to mind when you think of the word *loyal*? Who is the most loyal person you know?
- To whom are you most loyal? How do you demonstrate that loyalty?
- Do you seek Jesus for who he is or for what you can get out of him? Are there areas of your spiritual life where you're focused more on yourself than on God?

❏ **Day 5 (Hands):** Make a list of your top ten prayers—what you want from God. Now go back and circle those that are more for your comfort than for God's glory.

25

Can Jesus Help Me See Clearly?

Biblical Concept: Clarity
Read: John 9:1–41

For twenty-two years I was a professor of New Testament at Ozark Christian College in Joplin, Missouri. It was a great season with many fond memories. However, there was one thing that annoyed me. Bible college students would sometimes get bitten by the theology bug. They became enamored with "deep mysteries." Their debates did more to boost bloated egos than to lift the lost. What you're about to read is one such conversation that took place in Jesus's day.

The Southern Steps

If you go to Jerusalem today, on the south side of the Temple Mount, you can stand on the very steps where Jesus met a blind beggar. There the disciples asked, "Rabbi, who sinned, this man or his parents, that he was born blind?" (John 9:2). Why would they ask that?

One possibility is that they got bitten by the theology bug. They asked about this idea that sickness was caused by sin (Job 4:7; 8:20). *Wait a minute,* you might be thinking. *He was* born *blind. Could he sin in the womb?* Yes, actually, according to some of the rabbis. They would point to Jacob, who came out of the womb holding on to his brother's heel (Genesis 25:22–26). They taught that Jacob attempted to kill his brother in the womb.

Even worse, they taught that a parent's sin could result in a child's blindness. For this they referenced the Ten Commandments: "I the LORD your God am a jealous God, visiting the iniquity of the fathers on the children to the third and the fourth generation of those who hate me" (Exodus 20:5).

Jesus set things straight: "It was not that this man sinned, or his parents, but that the works of God might be displayed in him" (John 9:3). In other words, the blindness would result in God being glorified. They were asking "Why?" "Why" questions are about causes and ultimately lead to frustration. In contrast, Jesus asked "Who?" Who needs help? Who needs healing? And who can provide it?

Our role as Christ followers is to bring help and healing, not just answers to theological questions. Let's keep that in mind. This story is a mirror to see ourselves and a window to see our world.

The Pool of Siloam

Jesus spit on the ground to make a little mud and rubbed it on the man's eyes. Weird! People back then believed that a person's saliva could have healing properties. In short, Jesus was healing the blind man in a way he could understand. Then Jesus said, "Go, wash in the pool of Siloam" (verse 7). *Siloam* means "sent." So, the man was sent to "Sent" to wash!

As soon as he could see, he headed home. Imagine seeing for the first time! His neighbors noticed the delight on his face and said, "Is this not the man who used to sit and beg?" (verse 8). Some said, "Yes," but others assumed he was someone who looked similar. He actually had to defend his identity: "I am the man" (verse 9).

He told them, "The man called Jesus made mud and anointed my eyes and said to me, 'Go to Siloam and wash.' So I went and washed and received my sight" (verse 11). You would think they would have celebrated, but no. The very mention of Jesus set off warning sirens in their heads. That was the man their leaders had attempted to arrest (7:30, 32, 44) and kill (8:59). They knew the penalty of aligning with him: excommunication (9:22).

The Trial

The neighbors turned the ex-blind man over to a group of religious leaders who asked him how it had happened. He repeated the same story. These leaders were convinced Jesus was a sinner for working on the Sabbath. But they asked, " 'How can a man who is a sinner do such signs?' And there was a division among them" (verse 16).

Next, the Pharisees interrogated the man's parents: "Is this your son, who *you say* was born blind?" (verse 19). These leaders acted like it was all a big scam! His parents affirmed that he was, in fact, their son, but they had no idea how he had been healed.

This led to a *third* interrogation. They brought the man back in and said, "Give glory to God. We know that this man is a sinner" (verse 24). In other words, they told him to credit God alone with the miracle since Jesus was a sinner. His reply shows how clearly he saw: "Whether he is a sinner I do not know. One thing I do know, that though I was blind, now I see" (verse 25). The discussion ended quickly. The man was kicked out.

Jesus went to find him. "Do you believe in the Son of Man?" he asked (verse 35). The man's answer is a model for us: "Who is he, sir, that I may believe in him?" (verse 36). In other words, "You tell me who to believe in, and I will." When someone gives you sight, you should listen to him. The man confessed, "Lord, I believe," and he worshipped Jesus (verse 38). Then when Jesus said, "For judgment I came into this world, that those who do not see may see, and those who see may become blind," some of the Pharisees overheard and said, "Are we also blind?" (verses 39–40). Jesus answered, "If you were blind, you would have no guilt; but now that you say, 'We see,' your guilt remains" (verse 41).

Here's the warning for us: When you think you can see, you might be blind. When you know you're blind, Jesus can give you sight. As he said, "I am the light of the world. Whoever follows me will not walk in darkness, but will have the light of life" (8:12).

Key Points

- Spiritual arrogance will make you blind. You may sound smart, but you'll miss Jesus.

- The healing of the blind man is a reflection of our own spiritual journeys from darkness to light.

- We don't need to prove *everything* we believe about Jesus so long as we're clear about this *one thing:* once I was blind, but now I see.

This Week

❏ **Day 1 (Eyes):** After reading the essay, answer this question: Are you in danger of spiritual arrogance?

❏ **Day 2 (Ears):** Read 2 Samuel 22. How did David use the metaphor of darkness and light to refer to God's saving work? Bonus question: Where else do we find this poem?

❏ **Day 3 (Heart):** What do these verses teach you about spiritual light and spiritual blindness: 2 Corinthians 4:6, Ephesians 1:18, and Revelation 3:17?

❏ **Day 4 (Voice):** Discussion:

- How is darkness portrayed in movies and other popular media? What does it represent?
- What was the darkest day of your life? The brightest day of your life?
- Do people in the dark know they're in the dark? Why do people in the dark think people in the light are blind? Overachiever challenge: Read the allegory of the cave in Plato's *Republic.*
- Do you know of areas of your life where you don't think or see clearly? How does spiritual arrogance cause blindness?

❏ **Day 5 (Hands):** Ask someone who knows you well and whom you trust as wise (whether Christian or not) what your blind spots might be.

26

Can Jesus Accept Me?

Biblical Concept: Liberation
Read: Matthew 12:22–45

Here's an email I got today: "I was baptized when I was thirteen and got involved with the ministry. However, by my senior year in high school, I had completely walked away from my faith. After a few years and many mistakes, I've now felt compelled to return to Jesus. Which brings me to my first question: How does God make things happen in my life if He allows free will? My second question is much more straightforward and is likely part of the reason I left the church: Dinosaurs?"

Her two questions may seem unrelated. But it's actually a logical sequence. First, she fell prey to Satan's scheme of calling good evil and evil good. The world promised her freedom but gave her bondage, regret, and shame. Next, she wonders whether God can welcome her back. Last, as for her question about dinosaurs, it's a question about science contradicting the Bible. But the real question she needs to wrestle with is whether Jesus rose from the dead. Each of these three points plays out in today's text.

1. Calling Good Evil and Evil Good

A blind, mute, and demonized man was healed by Jesus. The man began to speak and see. The miracle was undeniable. But as we saw in chapter 10, the Pharisees said, "It is only by Beelzebul, the prince of demons, that this man casts out demons" (Matthew 12:24). Beelzebul, a synonym for Satan, was an ancient Canaanite deity.

However, Jesus pointed out, "Every kingdom divided against itself is laid waste, and no city or house divided against itself will stand. And if Satan casts out Satan, he is divided against himself. How then will his kingdom stand?" (verses 25–26). In short, "If I'm destroying Satan's house from within, why worry?"

Jesus continued, "I'm breaking and entering on Satan's turf; I've bound the strong man, and you stand against me. You'd better *back off*!" This was serious trash talk: "Whoever is not with me is against me" (verse 30). They suggested Jesus should be feared because he did the devil's work. Jesus said, "No, *you* should be terrified because I'm doing God's work and you oppose me." If Jesus could bind Satan, imagine what he could do to us.

2. Can God Receive Me Back?

At some point, all of us have asked that question. Addiction, deceit, abuse, sexual misconduct, greed, pride, and many other experiences can leave us feeling unworthy of God. Jesus addressed this directly: "Every sin and blasphemy will be forgiven people, but the blasphemy against the Spirit will not be forgiven . . . either in this age or in the age to come" (verses 31–32). When people are overwhelmed with guilt and shame, they sometimes ask, "Have I blasphemed the Holy Spirit? Have I gone too far? Am I unsavable?" Take a deep breath. An illustration might help.

Imagine you've fallen down a cliff and caught hold of a rope draped from the top. It has several knots to help you climb back up. Each knot represents a gift from God that could save you from falling to your death.

One knot is nature, through which God has revealed himself. Other knots include prophecies to warn us, miracles to get our attention, Jesus to preach truth, and the Holy Spirit to convict us. These Pharisees had rejected everything God gave that pointed to Jesus. They even rejected Jesus himself. Their last hope on this rope was the conviction of the Holy Spirit. If they rejected the Spirit, there was nothing else to hold on to.

What about you? Have you committed the unforgivable sin? No, not if you're asking the question. If you want to be saved, it's because the Spirit is calling you. He hasn't abandoned you, which means you haven't fully and finally rejected him. Anyone who *wants* to be saved has hope to be saved.

3. Smoke Screens and Resurrection

Whenever someone asks me for evidence for faith, I ask, "Do you *want* to believe?" If you want to believe, there's enough evidence. If you don't want to believe, no amount of miracles will convince you.

The scribes and Pharisees responded, "Teacher, we wish to see a sign from you" (verse 38). He had just performed an exorcism! Wasn't that enough? Actually, no.

Jesus said to them, "An evil and adulterous generation seeks for a sign, but no sign will be given to it except the sign of the prophet Jonah. For just as Jonah was three days and three nights in the belly of the great fish, so will the Son of Man be three days and three nights in the heart of the earth" (verses 39–40). The only sign Jesus offered was his own resurrection.

If that doesn't convince you, nothing will (Luke 16:31). If the Resurrection *does* convince you, nothing else matters—not dinosaurs, tragedies, philosophies, politics, or other religions.

If you want to believe, then believe now. Don't procrastinate; don't hesitate; don't waver. Give your allegiance to Jesus. If you don't, you may find yourself wandering in the wilderness, far from God. You may doubt your ability to be saved (or God's willingness to save you). Or worse, you may actually pass the last knot on the rope of hope, find that the Holy Spirit has abandoned you, and forget what it's like to want to believe.

Key Points

- When you call good evil and evil good, some very bad things can happen in your life.

- The blasphemy of the Holy Spirit is the full and final rejection of the Spirit's promptings toward faith in Jesus. If you want to believe, you haven't blasphemed the Spirit, since that desire comes from him.

- The resurrection of Jesus is the only sufficient evidence for faith. If you believe in that, nothing else matters; if you don't believe in that, nothing else can convince you.

This Week

☐ **Day 1 (Eyes):** After reading the essay, answer this question: Are you in bondage to guilt, shame, or doubt?

☐ **Day 2 (Ears):** Read the book of Jonah. How does his story prefigure Jesus's life, death, and resurrection?

☐ **Day 3 (Heart):** Think about Hebrews 6:4–6, Hebrews 10:26, and 1 John 5:16. What do these passages say about willful unbelief?

☐ **Day 4 (Voice):** Discussion:
- Have you ever doubted your salvation?
- Have you ever put up an intellectual smoke screen—a difficult question or an apparent contradiction in the Bible—as an excuse for unbelief? Have you had a friend do that as you were sharing your faith?
- The Pharisees had a hidden motive for not believing in Jesus. What are some hidden motives that have kept you, your friends, or your family away from faith? Why did Jesus make his own resurrection the focal point of faith? Why is it such a big deal?
- What are some ways you have resisted the promptings of the Spirit?

☐ **Day 5 (Hands):** Pray this prayer for five days straight: *Holy Spirit, show me what your next step is in my faith journey.* Share with a mentor or friend what you believe the Holy Spirit is saying to you.

Section 3

The Preaching of Jesus

Jesus's preaching was mind blowing. Crowds came to hear his **teaching,** which laid out new rules for life. His **stories** (what we call parables) described the kingdom he intended to establish using the most innocent and engaging metaphors, but they turned the people's expectations on their head. Then there was his **training,** primarily reserved for insiders, coaching them how to carry out his mission.

> **Teaching:** chapters 27–30
> **Stories:** chapters 31–34
> **Training:** chapters 35–39

27

What Did Jesus Say About Social Justice?

Biblical Concept: Justice
Read: Luke 4:16–30

When I was a senior in high school, my pastor asked me to preach one Sunday evening. The audience was small but very encouraging. I remember thinking, *This is going to be a powerful message! I have so much to say.* Well, neither turned out to be the case. Compare that with Jesus's first recorded message in his hometown synagogue. His sermon was significant, and his audience was *not* encouraging. After it was over, they tried to execute him. What Jesus said two thousand years ago is still earth shattering. Let's listen in.

Homecoming

Jesus had been away from his hometown, Nazareth, for the better part of a year. He had gone off and gotten baptized by John the Baptist. He had gathered disciples, performed miracles, and even gotten an interview with Nicodemus, a member of the ruling court of Israel. It was quite a résumé for someone from the hills of Galilee.

Only Luke recorded this message. He wasn't so interested in the synagogue or Jewish culture in general. He was Greek after all. Rather, what mattered to Luke was the content of the message. Jesus's sermon set the course for the gospel's expansion: the good news would spread beyond the boundaries of Israel! It would eventually have an impact on Luke himself. This is the Great Commission in its infancy.

Synagogue Sermon

In a synagogue service, the text for the sermon was selected by the preacher of the day: a trained rabbi, an elder of the community, or an important visitor like Jesus.

Jesus deliberately rolled the scroll to Isaiah 61 and read verses 1–2. He picked this passage because it described his role as the Messiah:

> The Spirit of the Lord is upon me,
>> because he has anointed me
>> to proclaim good news to the poor.
> He has sent me to proclaim liberty to the captives
>> and recovering of sight to the blind,
>> to set at liberty those who are oppressed,
> to proclaim the year of the Lord's favor. (Luke 4:18–19)

This text includes three key claims that Jesus applied to himself. First, he was led by the Spirit of God. He was claiming God's guidance and authority. Second, his ministry was about compassion, specifically for the poor, captive, blind, and oppressed. This contradicts what the Jews had read about the Messiah in their literature. Rather than wreaking havoc on his enemies, Jesus would suffer for them. He would turn enemies into allies.

The final claim Jesus made was that he would bring about Jubilee (Leviticus 25:8–55). God commanded Israel to celebrate Jubilee every fifty years. All debts would be canceled. Just as the Sabbath was a day of rest each week, so Jubilee was a restoration after forty-nine years (seven times seven). Problem: this command of God was *never* practiced. There's no evidence that Israel ever enacted this law. Jesus did, though, spiritually. Through his death for his enemies, all debts were paid.

Audience Reaction

When Jesus finished reading, he said, "Today this Scripture has been fulfilled in your hearing" (Luke 4:21). His statement certainly caught the attention of the congregation. Imagine your pastor reading a portion of Revelation and saying, "That's me! I'm the fulfillment of this prophecy."

Their reaction was about what you would expect. They were impressed with his speaking ability, but they certainly didn't believe in him as the Messiah. After all, they knew this kid as the son of a day laborer. They knew his place in their world—or so they thought.

Jubilee Extends to Outsiders

Because his own people rejected him, Jesus promised that Jubilee would extend to outsiders who would be more receptive to his ministry.

He gave two illustrations to prove his point. Elijah was the most famous of all the prophets of the Old Testament. He raised a widow's son in Zarephath *outside* Israel (1 Kings 17:8–24). Elijah's protégé was Elisha, the only person (other than Jesus) to heal someone with leprosy. However, the man he healed, Naaman, was a military commander in Aram, *outside* Israel (2 Kings 5:1–14). Both major prophets did notable miracles for foreigners. The point Jesus was making is that God has always been interested in outsiders, and outsiders have always been interested in God.

This story offers three major insights into the Great Commission. First, the expansion to the ends of the earth was always Jesus's intention. God's goal has always been global! Second, the preaching of the truth isn't enough. We must also release captives, relieve sickness, and reduce debts. It's impossible to care for people's spiritual condition without attention to their physical difficulties. Third, the concern for social justice almost always results in hostility. The episode ends with this shocking response:

"When they heard these things, all in the synagogue were filled with wrath. And they rose up and drove him out of the town and brought him to the brow of the hill on which their town was built, so that they could throw him down the cliff. But passing through their midst, he went away" (Luke 4:28–30).

Going to outsiders typically creates resentment. It's part of the cost of being disciples of Jesus. If we aren't ready for that, we dare not claim to be his disciples. If we don't announce good news to the poor, we aren't fulfilling the commission of Jesus. We may just find him passing through our midst.

Key Points

- Jesus's first recorded sermon in Nazareth was his first Great Commission.

- Jesus always intended for the good news to go to the ends of the earth.

- The gospel isn't just the message of eternal salvation; it's social justice to the least and the lost.

This Week

❏ **Day 1 (Eyes):** After reading the essay, answer this question: Do you share Jesus's concern about social justice?

❏ **Day 2 (Ears):** Read the story of Elijah and the widow (1 Kings 17:8–24) and the story of Elisha and Naaman (2 Kings 5:1–14). How do they set an expectation of the kind of ministry Jesus would provide?

❏ **Day 3 (Heart):** Think about Acts 13:46, Romans 1:16, and Romans 2:9–10. Why did the good news of Jesus go to the Jews first and then to the rest of the world?

❏ **Day 4 (Voice):** Discussion:
- Have you personally experienced what Jesus said: "No prophet is acceptable in his hometown" (Luke 4:24)? Why do you think that is?
- What happens when a church is concerned about spiritual needs and not social justice? What happens when a church is more concerned about social justice than spiritual needs?
- What makes a church welcoming to outsiders? What could we do better to make outsiders feel welcome?
- On a scale of 1 to 10, how well are you fulfilling these two sides of the Great Commission? How could you improve in one of these areas?
  1. Sharing the truth about Jesus
  2. Showing the compassion of Jesus

❏ **Day 5 (Hands):** Schedule a time this week either to share the truth about Jesus with someone you know well or to show the compassion of Jesus to someone you don't know well.

28

What Did Jesus Say About Morality?

Biblical Concept: Ethics
Read: Matthew 5:3–48

True genius takes the complex and puts it on a bumper sticker that the rest of us can understand. Albert Einstein did that with the theory of relativity: $E = mc^2$ ("energy equals mass times the speed of light squared"). That simple equation changed physics. It wasn't that physics textbooks just added an appendix; they had to be completely rewritten.

What Einstein was to physics, Jesus was to ethics—only to a far greater degree. What Einstein did for science once in his life, Jesus did for religion *five times* in a single message that takes only seventeen minutes to recite. Here are the five ways Jesus changed ethics forever.

I. Reversal of Values

This sermon opens with what we call the Beatitudes. These short stanzas turn the values of the world on their head. Rather than the rich, the powerful, and the healthy being blessed, it's the poor, the powerless, and the persecuted.

Yet there's one beatitude—and only one—that Jesus expanded on:

"Blessed are those who are persecuted for righteousness' sake, for theirs is the kingdom of heaven" (Matthew 5:10). He made it personal: "Blessed are you when others revile you and persecute you and utter all kinds of evil against you falsely *on my account*" (verse 11). Jesus didn't talk about suffering for your country, religion, or ethnic group. Suffering for *him* was the new blessing.

Jesus concluded the sermon with the parable of the wise man building his house on the rock (7:24–27). That rock is *his words*. He is the new law. Jesus himself is the measure of ethics. So righteousness now requires a relationship. This idea is unbelievably brilliant and can fit in a tweet.

The poor know they need Jesus. They realize they have no hope on their own. So they call on God. And he answers them. The rich, on the other hand, often trust their own power or success. This illusion of self-sufficiency will damn good people to hell. The kingdom of Christ is upside down. All you really need is nothing. Because then you call on Jesus for everything.

2. Behavior to Motives

Here's the second major shift in ethics: "I tell you, unless your righteousness exceeds that of the scribes and Pharisees, you will never enter the kingdom of heaven" (Matthew 5:20). How in the world is that possible? The Pharisees prayed twice a day, fasted once a week, and tithed their garden herbs.

Who can top that? Fortunately, Jesus isn't asking you to obey more rules. Instead, he demands better motives. He shifted ethics from your hands to your heart. Here are six specific illustrations he gave:

The Law Says	Jesus Says	Matthew 5
Don't murder.	Don't harbor anger.	21–26
Don't commit adultery.	Don't lust in your heart.	27–30

Offer a certificate of divorce.	Don't divorce except for adultery.	31–32
Don't break an oath.	Be completely honest.	33–37
Retaliate fairly.	Don't resist your opponent.	38–42
Love your neighbors.	Love your enemies.	43–48

Ethics focuses on behavior. Jesus focuses on motives. Many "righteous" people never break a command but still break hearts. A person can avoid murder but still destroy someone's reputation with gossip. You can avoid premarital sex but still fall prey to pornography. You can find a way to cheat on a test while not technically breaking a rule. But motives matter. If your motives are pure, your behavior will follow.

3. Love in Spite of, Not Because Of

One of these six commands stands out among the rest: "I say to you, Love your enemies and pray for those who persecute you" (Matthew 5:44). Jesus isn't telling us to feel warm and fuzzy toward those who hate us. He's ordering his followers to love their enemies with actions. Feed them if they're hungry. House them if they're homeless. This may be the most offensive thing Jesus ever said. Yet it has never been more needed than now. Mother Teresa, Mahatma Gandhi, and Martin Luther King Jr. demonstrated how sweeping social changes are possible through those who are willing to risk taking Jesus at his word. In the face of racism, terrorism, and tribalism, we need Christians to be true believers and live like Jesus knew what he was talking about. God help us if we don't.

4. God as Father

When Jesus teaches us to pray, it's in a brand-new way. We call it the Lord's Prayer (Matthew 6:9–13). It begins, "Our Father in heaven" (verse 9). Until Jesus, no one prayed like that. Jesus, however, *always* prayed to God as Father—except when he quoted Psalm 22 from the cross, "My

God, my God, why have you forsaken me?" (Mark 15:34). If we could just comprehend the connection we have with God through Jesus, it would radically improve our prayers (Matthew 7:11)!

The word *Father* is used *seventeen times* in this one sermon. It's one of the unique things about Christianity. We see the Creator of the universe as our Father!

5. From Silver to Gold

The final idea that radically altered ethics is found in one of the most familiar verses in the Bible: "Whatever you wish that others would do to you, do also to them, for this is the Law and the Prophets" (Matthew 7:12). On one hand this is familiar. As far back as Confucius, you can find this principle: "Don't do to others what you don't want done to you." This is known as the Silver Rule. But notice the slight variation Jesus made. He took the negative and made it positive in the Golden Rule: "Do to others . . ." That changes *everything.* The Silver Rule is passive. You can even do it on the beach. The Golden Rule is active. It requires effort *everywhere.*

Key Points

- Jesus is genius, putting earth-altering truth into bumper-sticker statements.
- Jesus's values turn the world's values upside down.
- Jesus altered ethics by shifting the focus from behavior to motives.

This Week

❑ **Day 1 (Eyes):** After reading the essay, answer this question: Which of these five alterations of ethics do you find most challenging?

❑ **Day 2 (Ears):** Read Exodus 20:1–17, the Ten Commandments. How would they be seen differently through the lens of Jesus's ethics?

❑ **Day 3 (Heart):** Think about Romans 13:9, Galatians 5:13, and 1 John 3:16–18. Christianity is based on love. How would you define love based on these passages?

❑ **Day 4 (Voice):** Discussion:
- Can you think of a time when someone kept the letter of the law but still violated the intention of the law? For example, a child can do exactly what his parents ask but have a hard and disobedient heart. Share an illustration.
- Would you say your church focuses more on the letter of the law or the intention of the law?
- Which of these five alterations of ethics do you think is most needed right now? Feel free to apply this to your family, your work, or society at large.
- Which of these five would you say you have the best understanding of? Which is most challenging for you?

❑ **Day 5 (Hands):** Pick a day this week (or perhaps just an hour), and try to perfectly live out the Golden Rule.

29

What Did Jesus Say About Religious Duties?

Biblical Concept: Piety
Read: Matthew 6:1–18

I remember praying in youth group. As my turn approached, I would begin mentally crafting my prayer, scripting it for my friends, not for God. By the time I said "Amen," I could imagine tears streaming from their eyes. Surely they would think, *If only I were as holy as he is.* How often do we all do something similar? Our efforts are not to please God but to impress people. That's why public piety (religious devotion) can be so dangerous. Jesus had an important warning about this.

The Problem with Piety

If our devotion is designed to impress people rather than God, it's selfish. Plain and simple. For example, instead of genuinely asking God for his help, we pray for others to overhear. We may sign up to serve not because we want to meet a need but because it looks good on a college application. We effectively put ourselves on the throne rather than God. Motives matter.

Jesus warns us, "Beware of practicing your righteousness before other people in order to be seen by them" (Matthew 6:1). Why? Because that's all you get. People see you. However, when God is your only audience, you get something much better. God rewards you. Which do you care more about? Praise from people or praise from God? We can choose only one. Jesus provided three illustrations to make the point: offerings, prayer, and fasting.

1. **Offerings:** "When you give to the needy, sound no trumpet before you, as the hypocrites do in the synagogues and in the streets, that they may be praised by others. Truly, I say to you, they have received their reward. But when you give to the needy, do not let your left hand know what your right hand is doing, so that your giving may be in secret. And your Father who sees in secret will reward you" (verses 2–4).

    Israel had no governmental social welfare system. The poor were primarily dependent on extended family. If they didn't have family, they were forced to rely on handouts. Those who provided for the poor announced it with trumpets. To be honest, historians aren't sure what Jesus was referring to. It might be the trumpet-shaped brass receptacles in the temple that clanged when coins were dropped in. Or it could be literal trumpets blown when money was given. While this seems like showing off, let's be real. We do the same thing with awards for those who give big to God's work. Public generosity is sometimes appropriate (Acts 4:36–37; 21:24; Philippians 4:14–18). However, it can become dangerous. Anonymous giving ensures that we get approval from God alone.

2. **Prayer:** "When you pray, you must not be like the hypocrites. For they love to stand and pray in the synagogues and at the street corners, that they may be seen by others. Truly, I say to you, they have received their reward. But when you pray, go into your room and shut the door and pray to your Father who is in

secret. And your Father who sees in secret will reward you" (Matthew 6:5–6).

Obviously, public prayer is perfectly appropriate (Acts 1:24; 3:1; 4:24). The problem is when prayer is used to speak to an earthly audience rather than our Father in heaven. We've all seen this, and probably most of us have done it.

If we speak to be heard by people, our praise will come from people. But when we speak directly to God, he will hear and answer regardless of others overhearing our conversation. Jesus offered a stellar example of how to pray in Matthew 6:9–13, which we call the Lord's Prayer. (See *Core 52 Student Edition*, chapter 20 for details on how to implement it in your own prayer life.)

3. **Fasting:** "When you fast, do not look gloomy like the hypocrites, for they disfigure their faces that their fasting may be seen by others. Truly, I say to you, they have received their reward. But when you fast, anoint your head and wash your face, that your fasting may not be seen by others but by your Father who is in secret. And your Father who sees in secret will reward you" (verses 16–18).

Fasting is a lost art. If you practice it, you know the powerful benefits of telling your body it isn't the boss. It's an effective spiritual discipline, but it becomes dangerous if done for public praise rather than private worship.

The law of Moses commanded one fast a year—the Day of Atonement. However, the Pharisees fasted every Tuesday and Thursday. Is it any coincidence that these two days were when the public markets were open? They wanted to prove their piety publicly. Which they did. And they were rewarded, but their reward came from their peers, not their God.

Conclusion

One of the deepest needs of human beings is approval. That need is embedded in us by God's design. The problem isn't our need for significance. It's where we look for it. God designed us to seek approval first from our parents. In turn, they can point us to our heavenly Father for approval. If we miss this, we will spend our lives in an endless pursuit of human praise. However, when we find approval from our heavenly Father, we find an ever-present and inexhaustible source of self-esteem. He will affirm you if you exercise your piety for his eyes only.

Key Points

- Piety (religious actions) performed for other people will lead to pride.

- Offerings, prayer, and fasting are examples of religious actions that can gain attention from God or from people. Whom you perform them for will determine whom you receive recognition from.

- God created us with a need for approval. Ultimately, he alone can meet that need.

This Week

❏ **Day 1 (Eyes):** After reading the essay, answer this question: Is your need for approval satisfied by God or others?

❏ **Day 2 (Ears):** Read 1 Samuel 13 and 17. How did King Saul and King David differ in seeking the approval of people versus God?

❏ **Day 3 (Heart):** Think about your need for approval in light of Galatians 1:10, Colossians 3:23, and 1 Thessalonians 2:4.

❏ **Day 4 (Voice):** Discussion:

- What percentage of people do you suppose have a healthy self-image? What are some of the indications that a person has low self-esteem? Often people who appear arrogant are actually insecure. How have you seen that revealed in your own experience?
- How can public acts of piety lead to hypocrisy?
- When are you most tempted to let people know of your religious devotion?
- When is it okay to publicly perform religious actions, and when does it become dangerous to your spiritual health?

❏ **Day 5 (Hands):** On a scale of 1 to 5 (1 being completely private and 5 being primarily public), rate the following religious practices in your own life: prayer, giving, Bible reading, church attendance, fasting (if applicable), volunteer service.

30

Why Does Jesus Care So Much About My Money?

Biblical Concept: Wealth
Read: Matthew 6:19–34

When I was twelve, my father began to give me a monthly allowance. It was a pretty good chunk of change for a kid, but I had to buy *everything* except food. Movies, clothes, video games—all my responsibility. He taught me how to make a budget and plan for the future.

More importantly, he taught me to give to God. Beginning when I was in first grade, if my father gave me a dime, he taught me to give a penny to the church. When it became a dollar, I set aside a dime for the offering. This taught me an important lesson: God owns everything! I'm just a steward of what God has given, which takes away pressure. The manager of the company always sleeps better than the owner. Stewards carry responsibility, but they don't need to worry. If you have high anxiety, what Jesus is about to teach about money can really help reduce it.

Principle 1: Our Hearts Follow Our Money

You like something, so you buy it. You like someone, so you get her a gift. Sometimes your money follows your heart. However, your heart *always* follows your money. If you spend money on shoes, video games, or clothes, those things will have your attention. That's why Jesus said, "Do not lay up for yourselves treasures on earth, where moth and rust destroy and where thieves break in and steal, but lay up for yourselves treasures in heaven, where neither moth nor rust destroys and where thieves do not break in and steal. *For where your treasure is, there your heart will be also*" (Matthew 6:19–21).

The apostle Paul would say it even more forcefully: "You may be sure of this, that everyone who is sexually immoral or impure, or who is *covetous (that is, an idolater),* has no inheritance in the kingdom of Christ and God" (Ephesians 5:5). Materialism is idolatry. It sounds extreme, but it's true. That's why tithing (giving our first 10 percent to the local church) is so important. It turns our hearts toward God. It establishes his ownership of everything.

Jesus made it clear: "No one can serve two masters, for either he will hate the one and love the other, or he will be devoted to the one and despise the other. You cannot serve God and money" (Matthew 6:24).

If you obsess over possessions, they become the objects of your affection. However, if you look to heaven, God will be your focus. We all have a choice about whom we will serve, but to quote Bob Dylan, "You're gonna have to serve somebody."[1] Follow the money, and you'll find your one true master.

Principle 2: Our Worry Reveals Our Worship

More money means less to worry about, right? Wrong! Wealth *increases* worry. Wealth doesn't eliminate worry; worship does! Now, we still work hard, save wisely, and spend carefully. But we also recognize God as the source of all our good. A right view of God allows a proper perspective on wealth, and *that* eliminates (or at least radically reduces) worry.

Jesus said, "I tell you, do not be anxious about your life, what you will eat or what you will drink, nor about your body, what you will put on. Is not life more than food, and the body more than clothing?" (verse 25). He offered two illustrations of why we shouldn't worry: birds and flowers. Neither has a care in the world, but they have all the care they need from God. Each chirp and every bloom declare God's constant provision.

God cares more about you than birds or flowers! How much more will he meet your physical, emotional, and spiritual needs? Do you believe that? Our anxiety says we don't!

No mental illness is more common in the US than anxiety disorders, which affect forty million adults each year. That's 18.1 percent of the population.[2] The US is one of the most anxious nations on earth.[3] Our wealth clearly hasn't reduced our worry. It's estimated that anxiety disorders cost the US $42 billion per year.[4] So it turns out Jesus was right not only theologically but also psychologically and economically.

Worry may increase our activity but never our productivity. As Jesus put it, "Which of you by being anxious can add a single hour to his span of life?" (verse 27). Modern medicine bears that out: worry actually decreases both the length and the quality of your life.

Worry is practical atheism. Unbelievers worry because they don't know the Father in heaven. Jesus said as much: "The Gentiles seek after all these things [food and clothing], and your heavenly Father knows that you need them all" (verse 32). To those of us who know the love of God, however, Jesus says, "Seek first the kingdom of God and his righteousness, and all these things will be added to you" (verse 33).

Conclusion

Humans tend to worry about two things: significance and provision. Because we need significance, we often perform religious duties for the audience around us rather than for God above us. Jesus's solution in Matthew 6:1–18 is to seek God's approval alone. God will certainly recognize those doing good for his sake. Likewise, we tend to worry about provision. Many of us are afraid we won't have enough. We hoard resources and are reluctant to be generous. Jesus's solution in Matthew 6:19–34 is to trust God for provision so we can be generous with those who need it most.

This one chapter deals with the two deepest needs of human beings in a way that promotes health, charity, and unity.

Key Points

- Our wealth is spiritual at the deepest level.
- Worry is practical atheism.
- Matthew 6 offers solutions to the two things we worry about most: significance and provision.

This Week

☐ **Day 1 (Eyes):** After reading the essay, how would you rate your own worry on a scale of 1 to 10? What does that reveal about where you need to grow in faith?

☐ **Day 2 (Ears):** Read the following proverbs on wealth: Proverbs 3:27; 6:6–8; 10:4; 11:25; 12:11; 13:11, 22; 14:23; 22:7, 9, 16, 26–27; 24:33–34; 27:23–24; and 28:27.

☐ **Day 3 (Heart):** Think about the dangers of wealth as you read Ephesians 5:5, 1 Timothy 6:17–19, and Hebrews 13:5.

☐ **Day 4 (Voice):** Discussion:
- Who is someone you respect for his generosity? How would you rate that person's worry?
- Why do you think America has some of the highest rates of worry?
- What could you do now and in the future to distribute to others the provisions God has entrusted you with?
- What are you worried about right now? It's okay to be honest. Pray for one another to reduce anxiety.

☐ **Day 5 (Hands):** What are your sources of money? Take 10 percent of that money, and start the habit of tithing to your local church. This is one of the most important disciplines for spiritual growth in *every* area of your life.

31

How Does Jesus Feel About Prodigals?

Biblical Concept: Prodigals
Read: Luke 15:11–32

After my parents' divorce, the three of us boys (ages eleven, twelve, and fourteen) had to decide whom to live with. My older brother lived with Mom. My younger brother and I stayed with Dad. It was heart wrenching. I kept going to church, and my faith followed suit. My older brother stopped going to church. If we put ourselves in this story, he would be the prodigal son, and I would be the one who stayed at home and faithfully served his father. Does that make me a better person? I would like to think so, but this parable tells a different story. I know how easy it is to get lost at home. As we'll see, we all need grace.

Setting the Scene

Jesus had been hanging out with the outcasts of his day—tax collectors, prostitutes, and scallywags. "The tax collectors and sinners were all drawing near to hear him. And the Pharisees and the scribes grumbled, saying, 'This man receives sinners and eats with them.' So he told them this parable" (Luke 15:1–3). Except it wasn't just one parable. It was three: a lost sheep, a lost coin, and a lost son.

Why three stories in a row? Because Jesus is serious about the spiritually lost being found. He loves the people that religious people tend to avoid. The parable of the prodigal son is really about *two* lost sons. One got lost abroad and one got lost at home. This is the longest of Jesus's parables. It's such a masterpiece that Charles Dickens said it was the greatest short story ever.

The Son Who Got Lost Abroad

You may know a young man who is fed up with his father. That's not uncommon. But this boy took it to another level! "Give me the share of property that is coming to me," he said (verse 12). Problem: the inheritance was supposed to be given *after the death of the father*. To Jewish ears it sounded like this: "Dad, drop dead and give me what's mine!"

If you know anything about the shame-honor culture of the Middle East, the answer would obviously be "#%@* no!" This foolish son would surely squander the inheritance, and the father would be the laughingstock of the village. You can imagine the shock when Jesus said, "He divided his property between them" (verse 12). What on earth was going on? The father in the parable represents God. The audience knew that. Jesus was portraying God as a foolish father who gave in to an insubordinate son. That was shocking!

What happened next is as predictable as the girl falling for the guy in a chick flick: "The younger son . . . squandered his property in reckless living" (verse 13). Hard times fall especially hard on hardheaded fools. When his money was gone, his "hired" friends disappeared. Then a severe famine hit. He was desperate. So desperate, in fact, that he latched on to a pig farmer and begged for work. That's about as low as a kosher Jewish boy can go.

One day, while feeding the pigs, he thought, *This slop doesn't look half-bad*. It was then that he came to his senses. He said to himself, "How many of my father's hired servants have more than enough bread, but I perish here with hunger! I will arise and go to my father, and I will say to him, 'Father, I have sinned against heaven and before you. I am no longer worthy to be called your son. Treat me as one of your hired servants'" (verses 17–19). He memorized his speech and set off for home.

His father saw him from a distance and *ran* to his son. In the Middle East, noblemen never run. That's what thieves and slaves do out of fear. Once again, Jesus was portraying God the Father as throwing caution and dignity to the wind—all because of his love for us. What a picture!

The father said, "Bring quickly the best robe, and put it on him, and put a ring on his hand, and shoes on his feet. And bring the fattened calf and kill it, and let us eat and celebrate. For this my son was dead, and is alive again; he was lost, and is found" (verses 22–24). The father lavished his son with these three signs of family honor. The signet ring gave him authority over family affairs. The robe and sandals set him apart from the household servants. The father had worried that his son was dead, but now he was alive at home. This metaphor of resurrection is all over the place in the Epistles (Romans 6:4, 9–11; 7:4; 8:10–11; Ephesians 2:5; Colossians 2:13) and marks the life of the believer.

The Son Who Got Lost at Home

The older, "faithful" son heard the party. When he realized it was for his runaway brother, who had shamed the family, he was furious! He said to his father, "Look, these many years I have served you, and I never disobeyed your command, yet you never gave me a young goat, that I might celebrate with my friends. But when this son of yours came, who has devoured your property with prostitutes, you killed the fattened calf for him!" (Luke 15:29–30).

Did the older brother ever enter the house to celebrate his brother's return? We don't know because the story isn't finished. Remember, it started in verses 1–2, when Jesus was confronted by the Pharisees for hanging out with sinners. The Pharisees were still there in the room.

Jesus's open-ended story was an invitation for them (the older brothers) to join the celebration of sinners who had come back home. We're never told whether they did. So the story remains open for you too. Will *you* join the celebration of those coming home to the Father? Is justice (or vengeance) more important than celebrating the lost being found? The ending is up to you. How will you finish it?

Key Points

- Rejoicing over the lost being found was so important to Jesus that he told a string of three parables about it.

- Prodigals are shocked when they return home and are accepted as sons and daughters.

- Sons or daughters lost at home are offended when prodigals return and have their dignity restored.

This Week

☐ **Day 1 (Eyes):** After reading the essay, answer this question: Are you more like the older brother or the younger brother?

☐ **Day 2 (Ears):** What can we learn from 2 Chronicles 7:11–22 about repentance and restoration?

☐ **Day 3 (Heart):** Think about what repentance looks like according to Acts 3:19, 2 Corinthians 7:9–10, and 1 Peter 2:25.

☐ **Day 4 (Voice):** Discussion:

- Have you known someone who was a prodigal who returned to her community of faith? What was that person's experience like? If it was you, share your story.
- Why do you think it's difficult for "older brothers" to welcome prodigals home?
- What could your church do to make prodigals feel more celebrated when they come home?
- What could you do personally to make a prodigal more open to attending church with you?

☐ **Day 5 (Hands):** Ask a prodigal you know well, "If you ever did decide to come back to church, what would make you feel welcome?"

32

How Do I Hear God's Voice?

Biblical Concept: Parables
Read: Matthew 13:1–23

Hearing loss is common as adults age. Higher-pitch frequencies especially become harder to hear. Many women have higher-pitch voices. As a man ages, he naturally has a harder time hearing his wife's voice. Uh-oh! That combination isn't always good for marriage. In the same way, over time, we can become deaf to the voice of God. And that isn't good for our spiritual health. The stories Jesus told helped some people hear better but made others tone deaf.

An Earthly Story with a Heavenly Meaning

Jesus was famous for his parables. He told a total of thirty-eight. We have over two thousand parables from other rabbis, but none of them predate Jesus. So it may well be that Jesus invented this teaching tool and others imitated him. Like the other parables, Jesus's stories involve stock metaphors. Masters, fathers, and kings represent God. Servants and children represent God's servants or prophets. A harvest stands for judgment, and a feast portrays the messianic banquet. Each of these metaphors represents something in real life. Some, in fact, believe that every time Jesus told a parable, he could have pointed to the objects he was speaking about right around him.

A couple of things set Jesus's parables apart. First, every other rabbi told parables to reinforce traditional values. Jesus used parables to explode expectations and teach something new. Second, other rabbis used parables to illustrate points in their messages. For Jesus, the parables *were* the message. Specifically, Jesus's parables were *all* about the kingdom of God. Matthew 13 is the greatest example of this. He told eight parables in a row. We'll focus on the first: the parable of the sower.

Parable of the Sower

This first story is about a farmer scattering his seed everywhere. Without modern technology, his best bet was to throw the seed wherever he could.

Some of it fell on the path that had been compacted by human footsteps, making it impenetrable. The birds (representing Satan, Mark 4:15) snatched the seed away. Some of the seed fell on shallow soil among the rocks. It sprang up quickly, but the lack of depth meant there was too little moisture to sustain growth. That's like persecution that causes some to quickly abandon their new faith. Other seed fell on soil with weed seed. They grew up together, but the weeds won out. These weeds represent life's worries, riches, and pleasures.

Some seed, however, fell on good soil and produced a hundredfold, sixtyfold, or thirtyfold. (A good yield was tenfold, so this is an exaggeration, common in parables.) The life lesson is this: All the soil is actually the same. The difference is what is added to it—stones, weeds, or a good stomping. That's what causes some to hear the message of the kingdom and others to go deaf to spiritual things. Furthermore, in the Bible, hearing implies obedience. Since Matthew 13:13–23 mentions hearing fourteen times, if you want to get into Jesus's kingdom, you don't just listen; you obey.

"Why Do You Speak to Them in Parables?"

No one understood what this story meant. Even Jesus's closest disciples. So they turned to him in the boat and asked, "Why do you speak to them in parables?" (verse 10). Jesus's answer was shocking: "To you it has been given to know the secrets of the kingdom of heaven, but to them it has not been given. For to the one who has, more will be given, and he will have an abundance, but from the one who has not, even what he has will be taken away. This is why I speak to them in parables, because seeing they do not see, and hearing they do not hear, nor do they understand." (verses 11–13).

Jesus basically said that parables make the kingdom clear to those who *want* to believe. Yet to those who reject Jesus, parables conceal the kingdom. That doesn't sound fair! Well, it's not fair. It is, however, reality. The most popular shoe brand makes a lot more money. Beautiful people make the cover of magazines. Star athletes get the best product endorsements. It's just the way life works. When it comes to the kingdom, however, the "blessed" are not those with good looks, amazing talents, or wealth. The blessed are those who believe. You may be one of them!

Jesus quoted ancient words from Isaiah. God told Isaiah to preach to the people of Jerusalem:

> "Keep on hearing, but do not understand;
> keep on seeing, but do not perceive."
> Make the heart of this people dull,
>   and their ears heavy,
>   and blind their eyes;
> lest they see with their eyes,
>   and hear with their ears,
> and understand with their hearts,
>   and turn and be healed. (Isaiah 6:9–10)

What on earth was going on here? Did God not want them to repent? Did He not want them to be saved? Well, of course he did. The problem wasn't with God. It was with them. Their persistent rejection showed their unwillingness to make God the Lord of their lives.

The more they listened to the message, the less they heard the message. It's like those who live under the flight path of an airport no longer hearing the planes. Those who live next to railroad tracks go deaf to trains. And those who go to church week after week but don't put into practice the truth of the gospel find themselves deaf to the Holy Spirit.

Spiritual sight is a great gift; it's not something to be wasted. As Jesus said, "Blessed are your eyes, for they see, and your ears, for they hear. For truly, I say to you, many prophets and righteous people longed to see what you see, and did not see it, and to hear what you hear, and did not hear it" (Matthew 13:16–17). If you are reading these words and want to believe, develop and protect that desire. It's a gift from God to be cherished and acted on.

Key Points

- Jesus told thirty-eight parables. All of them were about the kingdom of God.

- Parables are earthly stories with heavenly meanings.

- Parables reveal the kingdom to those who have faith but conceal it from those who reject the opportunity to believe.

This Week

☐ **Day I (Eyes):** After reading the essay, answer this question: Do you have eyes to see and ears to hear?

☐ **Day 2 (Ears):** Read Isaiah 6. How can we lose our spiritual sight and hearing?

☐ **Day 3 (Heart):** Think about Acts 28:26–27, Romans 11:8, and 2 Corinthians 3:14. What actions or attitudes make someone spiritually hard of hearing?

☐ **Day 4 (Voice):** Discussion:

- What makes people spiritually hard of hearing?
- Do you think you've always been a good listener when hearing the gospel? When did you listen more carefully, and when were you harder of hearing? What made the difference?
- Do you have a friend who is hard toward the gospel? Which kind of soil would you relate your friend to, and what could you do to help him hear the gospel?
- Brainstorm ideas for the day 5 exercise. Use your creativity to help each person come up with a story line.

☐ **Day 5 (Hands):** Sit down this week, and write a parable about hearing or seeing—an earthly story with a heavenly meaning.

33

How Can I Be Sure
I'm Saved?

Biblical Concept: Bias
Read: Luke 10:25–37

Yesterday I got an email asking how someone can be sure she is saved. It went something like this: "I attend church. I read my Bible. I pay my tithes. I volunteer. But I just feel like something is missing. How can I be *sure* I'm saved?" She listed all the good things she's doing to impress God. But she's forgetting that God is already impressed with us! We are his creation, his children. Like a mother loves her kids, our heavenly Father loves us. In fact, he loved us so much, he sent his Son to die for our sins. And it's Jesus's death, not our performance, that ensures our salvation. So, the question is not whether God loves us but whether we love him back. That's what the encounter with Jesus in Luke 10 is all about. Have you ever asked, "How can I be sure I'm saved?" This story answers that question clearly.

Question 1: The Query—How Are We Saved?

A lawyer came to Jesus with a question: "Teacher, what shall I do to inherit eternal life?" (verse 25). This man knew the Bible well. Jesus, using a common rabbinic teaching technique, answered his question with a question: "What is written in the Law? How do you read it?" (verse 26).

"Well," said the man, combining Deuteronomy 6:5 and Leviticus 19:18, "you shall love the Lord your God with all your heart and with all your soul and with all your strength and with all your mind, and your neighbor as yourself" (Luke 10:27). That was spot on. We know we're saved when we love God and demonstrate it by loving God's other children, our neighbors. It was a great answer.

Jesus replied, "Do this, and you will live" (verse 28). But looking for a loophole, the lawyer asked, "Who is my neighbor?" (verse 29). In pure Jesus fashion, he answered the question with a story.

Question 2: The Justification— Who Is My Neighbor?

"Once upon a time," said Jesus, "a man went down from Jerusalem to Jericho." This seventeen-mile stretch of highway was so dangerous that it was known as the Road of Blood. It was crawling with bandits.

Somewhere along the way, bandits attacked the man. They beat him and left him for dead. Before long, a priest walked by. He had probably been at the temple for one of his biannual weeks of service and was returning home to his family and work. He walked right by his fellow Israelite, likely assuming he was already dead. Some have noted that a priest was not to touch a dead body or he would become ritually unclean. While that's true, this priest was *leaving* Jerusalem. His duties were over. He would have had more than enough time for ritual cleansing. His fellow Israelite needed him now! Clearly, his motives were *not* pure. Perhaps he was afraid the bandits were still nearby, or worse, he might have simply not cared, justifying his inaction as many of us do: *What difference could I make?*

After the priest came a Levite. Same song, second verse. He walked by, distancing himself by crossing to the other side of the road. Then came a Samaritan. We call this story the parable of the good Samaritan, but if you scour the text, the word *good* isn't there. Why? Because there was no such thing as a good Samaritan, according to the Jews. There was bad blood between the two groups.

For example, in 128 BC, John Hyrcanus, a Jewish patriot, destroyed the Samaritan temple. The Samaritans retaliated by sneaking human bones into the Jerusalem temple at night and scattering them to defile the sanctuary. Samaritans were forbidden from testifying in a Jewish court of law because you had to be human to do so. And on it went. As you can imagine, *good Samaritan* was an oxymoron to the Jews.

The hatred of Samaritans was widespread, even among Jesus's disciples. One chapter earlier (Luke 9:51–54), Jesus passed through Samaria on his way to Jerusalem. When the locals refused to house the disciples, James and John said, "Lord, do you want us to tell fire to come down from heaven and consume them?" (verse 54). Whoa. That's aggressive!

Nonetheless, against all expectations, *this* Samaritan had compassion. "He went to him and bound up his wounds, pouring on oil and wine [which had medicinal value]. Then he set him on his own animal and brought him to an inn and took care of him. And the next day he took out two denarii [two days' wages] and gave them to the innkeeper, saying, 'Take care of him, and whatever more you spend, I will repay you when I come back'" (Luke 10:34–35). He might not have liked the Jewish man, but he loved him with action.

Question 3: The Test—Who Was Neighborly?

Jesus concluded the parable with a question: "Which of these three, do you think, proved to be a neighbor to the man who fell among the robbers?" (verse 36). Jesus was asking, "Who *became* a neighbor?" The lawyer wanted to know who his neighbors were—those he was *required* to love. Jesus said, "Go *be* a neighbor to whomever you see." Your neighbor is anyone within your reach!

There was only one right answer, and the lawyer knew it: "the one who showed him mercy." Jesus replied, "You go, and do likewise" (verse

37). With this, Jesus answered both questions: "Who is my neighbor?" (verse 29) and "What shall I do to inherit eternal life?" (verse 25). Jesus's answer hasn't changed. We prove our love for God by loving our neighbors. All of them.

Key Points

- We prove our love for God by showing love to fellow humans.

- Your neighbors are those within your reach. So whomever you come in contact with is your neighbor.

- The better question is not "Who is my neighbor?" but "Who is neighborly?"

This Week

❏ **Day 1 (Eyes):** After reading the essay, answer this question: Are you neighborly?

❏ **Day 2 (Ears):** Read the context of these two great commands in Deuteronomy 6 and Leviticus 19:9–18.

❏ **Day 3 (Heart):** Think about 1 John 3:15–16; 4:16–21; and 5:13. Based on these passages, how would you answer the question, "How can I be sure I'm saved?"

❏ **Day 4 (Voice):** Discussion:

- Who is the best neighbor you've ever had? Any stories of a really bad neighbor?
- Why do you think we can't love God without loving our neighbors?
- What do you think you would have done if you were the priest or Levite in the story?
- Do you have a harder time loving some people than others? Do you find it harder to love people when they trigger you with certain behaviors?

❏ **Day 5 (Hands):** Find one opportunity to make life easier for someone who isn't like you and who can't repay you.

34

How Did Jesus Lead?

Biblical Concept: Leadership
Read: John 10:1–21

Growing up, I wanted to be a brain surgeon. My motives weren't entirely pure. The prestige of the occupation was attractive. I suppose that's what drives most little boys and girls to their dream jobs—firefighter, doctor, astronaut, superhero.

In Jesus's day, boys didn't have dream jobs. They couldn't. They inherited their occupations from their fathers. But even if they did dream, no one dreamed of being a shepherd. Shepherds were often touching blood and dead animals. This made them ritually unclean. Furthermore, sheep grazed through other people's property. So anything that went missing was blamed on the boys leading the sheep. Not to mention that cute farmers' daughters often led to bad blood with the locals.

The Lord Is My Shepherd

The strange thing about shepherds in the Bible is that the *idea* of a shepherd was noble even if actual shepherds were shunned. In fact, God himself is described as the perfect shepherd: "The LORD is my shepherd; I shall not want" (Psalm 23:1). This idea is all over the place in the Old Testament! "He is our God, and we are the people of his pasture, and the sheep of his hand" (Psalm 95:7). "He will tend his flock like a shepherd; he will gather the lambs in his arms" (Isaiah 40:11). There are hosts of others (Genesis 48:15; Psalm 28:9; 78:52; 79:13; 80:1; 107:41; Ecclesiastes 12:11; Jeremiah 31:10; Ezekiel 34:15; Zechariah 9:16).

Virtually every major leader of Israel was a shepherd by occupation. Their time in the fields prepared them to lead the nation. David, for example, was the greatest king of Israel.

> [God] chose David his servant
>> and took him from the sheepfolds;
> from following the nursing ewes he brought him
>> to shepherd Jacob his people,
>> Israel his inheritance.
> With upright heart he shepherded them
>> and guided them with his skillful hand. (Psalm 78:70–72)

Likewise, for forty years Moses led Israel through the desert, where he had already spent four decades leading sheep (Exodus 3:1; Psalm 77:20; Isaiah 63:11). Before Moses there was Jacob (Genesis 29), and before Jacob, his grandfather Abraham (Genesis 13:5–7). This is the who's who of Israel's founding fathers. When Jesus claimed to be the shepherd of Israel, therefore, it was a political claim.

Jesus Is the Good Shepherd

John 10 is a gloves-off, no-holds-barred, heavyweight fight. Jesus stood in the temple, face to face with the "shepherds" of Israel. He accused them of being illegitimate, even satanic, while he is the one true shepherd of Israel. He said, "Truly, truly, I say to you, he who does not enter the sheepfold by the door but climbs in by another way, that man is a thief and a robber" (John 10:1).

This was nothing new. In the same way, centuries before, God criticized the religious leaders through his prophet Ezekiel: "Ah, shepherds of Israel . . . you eat the fat, you clothe yourselves with the wool, you slaughter the fat ones, but you do not feed the sheep" (34:2–3). His critique concluded with a promise: "I will set up over them one shepherd, my servant David, and he shall feed them: he shall feed them and be their shepherd" (verse 23).

The crowds were divided. Both Jesus and the Jewish leaders claimed to be shepherds of Israel. The chief priests and teachers of the law had been their recognized leaders all their lives. But Jesus performed unprecedented miracles. This caused many to conclude, "These are not the words of one who is oppressed by a demon. Can a demon open the eyes of the blind?" (John 10:21). Could he be the promised shepherd from Ezekiel 34?

How could the crowds determine whether his claim was valid? Jesus offered a series of tests for the true shepherd:

- **He knows his sheep.** The sheep recognize the voice of the shepherd (John 10:3–5, 14–16). Unlike shepherds in other parts of the world who drive their sheep, Palestinian shepherds call their sheep. Each one has a name, and the shepherd knows them all.

- **He sacrifices himself for his sheep.** The shepherd lays down his life for the sheep (verses 9, 11, 15, 17–18). In verse 9, Jesus said, "I am the door." The sheep pen was simply a low rock enclosure with an opening on one side. It didn't actually have a door. Rather, when the sheep were put in the pen to sleep, the shepherd lay in the doorway. He was saying, "No one gets to my sheep except over my dead body." In Jesus's case, however, his dead body allowed us to enter God's protective fold. He laid down his life for us.

- **He improves the lives of his sheep.** Jesus said, "The thief comes only to steal and kill and destroy. I came that they may have life and have it abundantly" (verse 10). We saw false shepherds in action over the past few chapters of John. Remember how they treated the lame man in chapter 5, the woman caught in adultery in chapter 8, and the blind man in chapter 9. Jesus, however, healed, freed, and loved those abused by their own religious system.

These are the very tests we should use for leaders of our own day. Do they make your life better, or do they use you to make their own lives better? Do they sacrifice the sheep or sacrifice *for* the sheep? Do they know their sheep by being among them? Whether someone is a business owner, a CEO, a teacher, a coach, a parent, or a pastor, a true shepherd lives as Jesus did—for the benefit of those God has put under his care.

Key Points

- Shepherds have always been a symbol of godly leadership— from Yahweh, to the heroes of the Bible, to Jesus himself.

- Jesus's words in John 10 mirror the ancient prophecy of Ezekiel 34 that a new shepherd would come to feed the flock of God.

- The three tests of a good shepherd that Jesus introduced are still valid for testing good leadership today.

This Week

❏ **Day 1 (Eyes):** After reading the essay, identify your own flock, the people you have influence over.

❏ **Day 2 (Ears):** After reading Ezekiel 34, underline all the similarities between this passage and John 10.

❏ **Day 3 (Heart):** Think about Hebrews 13:20, 1 Peter 2:25, and 1 Peter 5:4. What do these passages add to our understanding of Jesus as a shepherd?

❏ **Day 4 (Voice):** Discussion:
- Who is the best leader you've ever had outside your own family?
- Why is knowing the flock so important for a leader? Do you feel like you're known by your leaders?
- How can you tell whether a leader is sacrificing for you or using you for her benefit?
- Identify one thing a leader is doing to make your life better.

❏ **Day 5 (Hands):** If you're serving at church or leading at school, work on learning the names of those you lead.

35

How Can We Share Our Faith Effectively?

Biblical Concept: Evangelism
Read: Matthew 10:1–42

In middle school I hung out with three guys. None of them were Christians. I felt obligated to tell them about Jesus, but I was afraid of rejection. Peer pressure is heavy! One day I came across Matthew 10:32–33: "Everyone who acknowledges me before men, I also will acknowledge before my Father who is in heaven, but whoever denies me before men, I also will deny before my Father who is in heaven."

Then I learned that the word *acknowledge* means "speak up." I remember thinking, *I'd better figure out this evangelism thing if Jesus takes it that seriously.* That's why Jesus provided practical guidelines for sharing our faith:

1. **Offer help.** When the apostles met real needs (verse 8), people were far more open to the message of the kingdom. You can do the same thing. Jesus has given you gifts and abilities—things you're naturally good at! Use them to benefit your community. Then use that platform to share about Jesus.

2. **Go in teams.** Jesus sent the apostles out in pairs. If you read verses 2–4 closely, you will notice each pair is identified between the semicolons. Fact-check it for yourself! This model was followed in the book of Acts. You should do the same. Team up with others to share the good news of Jesus.

3. **Be strategic.** Surprisingly, Jesus told the Twelve, "Go nowhere among the Gentiles" (Matthew 10:5). What? I thought we were to go to the ends of the earth. We are. However, it was too soon for that. They needed to go first to the places where they would have the greatest potential for success. You also should go first to the people and places most open to the gospel, unless the Holy Spirit directs you otherwise.

4. **Keep the main thing the main thing.** Often people want to debate about creation, other religions, or politics. Don't. Here's what Jesus told us to talk about: "Proclaim as you go, saying, 'The kingdom of heaven is at hand'" (verse 7). Talk about Jesus, specifically his death for our sins and resurrection to life.

5. **Keep your motives pure.** Jesus warned the Twelve, "You received without paying; give without pay" (verse 8). The only benefit we're seeking is the honor of Jesus. We don't share our faith with ulterior motives.

6. **Find the influencer.** Jesus said, "Whatever town or village you enter, find out who is worthy in it and stay there until you depart" (verse 11). Find an influencer who is open to the gospel (or at least to you). Then if that person comes to Christ, he will influence others to follow. It could be a leader at work, a fellow teammate, a classmate, or a social influencer.

7. **Know when to "fold 'em."** There comes a time when our words are wasted. If people are unreceptive, at some point you drop it. It takes discernment to know when to quit, but Jesus told us pretty clearly, "If anyone will not receive you or listen to your words, shake off the dust from your feet when you leave

that house or town" (verse 14). There's a time to take a stand (Acts 8:1; 16:37–40; 21:13) and a time to back off (8:1; 13:51; 14:6, 20).

8. **Be ready to suffer.** Preaching Christ makes people uncomfortable. They have to face their sin and confess their need for a savior. Some react negatively. If they mistreated Jesus, should we expect anything different? As he said, "A disciple is not above his teacher, nor a servant above his master" (Matthew 10:24). There are three principles to keep in mind. First, fear the judgment of God more than the violence of humans. While humans can kill the body, Jesus warns us that God "can destroy both soul and body in hell" (verse 28). Second, carry your cross: "Whoever does not take his cross and follow me is not worthy of me. Whoever finds his life will lose it, and whoever loses his life for my sake will find it" (verses 38–39). Third, finish the race: "The one who endures to the end will be saved" (verse 22; see Matthew 24:13; Mark 13:13; Hebrews 3:14; Revelation 2:26).

9. **Trust the Spirit.** We may find ourselves in situations where we don't have all the answers or even lack the courage to speak up. It is then that the Spirit in us can give us just the right words. "You will be dragged before governors and kings for my sake, to bear witness before them and the Gentiles. When they deliver you over, do not be anxious how you are to speak or what you are to say, for what you are to say will be given to you in that hour. For it is not you who speak, but the Spirit of your Father speaking through you" (Matthew 10:18–20). Believe it!

10. **Remember God's love.** Jesus said, "Are not two sparrows sold for a penny? And not one of them will fall to the ground apart from your Father. But even the hairs of your head are all numbered. Fear not, therefore; you are of more value than many sparrows" (verses 29–31). God loves us more than we can imagine! And not only does he love us; he also provides us with the

resources and protection we need to complete the commission he has given us. When anyone speaks up for Jesus, the Lord takes that personally.

Key Points

- Being a witness for Jesus requires speaking up for him.

- Jesus gives us specific guidelines about how to effectively bear witness to him.

- Our ultimate power to share our faith comes not from our skills, knowledge, or training but from the guidance of the Spirit and the love of God.

This Week

❏ **Day 1 (Eyes):** After reading the essay, answer this question: How well are you doing speaking up for Jesus?

❏ **Day 2 (Ears):** Read Exodus 3–4. God called Moses to speak with Pharaoh; he had all kinds of excuses why he couldn't. How many of Jesus's talking points can you find in this story?

❏ **Day 3 (Heart):** Think about Romans 10:9–10, Hebrews 13:15, and 1 Peter 3:15. What do these verses say about speaking up for Jesus?

❏ **Day 4 (Voice):** Discussion:

- Who told you about Jesus? What did that person do right? What could she have done better?
- We're all afraid to speak up for Jesus at some level. What do you think is the worst that can happen?
- Whom would you like to tell about Jesus? What is your main concern about how he might respond or what you might do to offend him?
- Which of the ten points do you need to work on to be more effective in speaking up for Jesus?

❏ **Day 5 (Hands):** Put into practice one or two of the ten points this week.

36

Do You Ever Doubt Your Doubts?

Biblical Concept: Resilience
Read: Matthew 11:2–11

We all have our doubts. The "whale" swallowing Jonah and the Virgin Birth are miracles that are scientifically difficult to believe. Exclusive statements that suggest Jesus is the *only* way to salvation are tough. Dinosaurs, what the Bible teaches about sex—you name it. It's easy to find a reason to doubt. If, however, you want to doubt your doubts, that's just as easy. Look to Jesus, and you'll find enough to hang on to during any season of doubt.

Doubt Your Doubts

John the Baptist was Jesus's forerunner. He announced Jesus as the coming Messiah. He also preached in the wilderness about sin and social injustice. One of his sermons was against King Herod because Herod had seduced his brother's wife and married her. Yikes! John condemned such immorality. Herod didn't take too kindly to John's negative press. Herod's wife was worse. She was so furious that she convinced her hubby to have John arrested and thrown into prison.

This prison was actually a dungeon in Herod's winter palace in the desert. John had been there for ten months with lots of time to think. Jesus turned out to be different than John had imagined. The Messiah, according to the prophecies, was to release prisoners (Isaiah 61:1). So, why was John sitting in a cell? He sent messengers ninety miles north to ask Jesus, "Are you *really* the Messiah, or should we look for someone else?"

We've all had those moments when Jesus doesn't meet our expectations. Perhaps it's the pain of a broken relationship. Maybe it's sickness or your parents' divorce. All of us have been there. Jesus's response isn't just for John; it's for all of us: "Go and tell John what you hear and see: the blind receive their sight and the lame walk, lepers are cleansed and the deaf hear, and the dead are raised up, and the poor have good news preached to them. And blessed is the one who is not offended by me" (Matthew 11:4–6).

Jesus simply described his ministry. His reply is pretty much a quote, combining Isaiah 35:5–6 and Isaiah 61:1. He was telling John, "I may not have freed you from prison, but look at my résumé." Here's where it gets really interesting. He added a statement to his quotation that isn't found in either Isaiah 35 or Isaiah 61: "the dead are raised up."

Jesus was saying to John, "I know where you are, and I know what is going to happen to you. I won't free you from prison, but I will raise you from the dead. I'm not what you expected; I am more than you imagined." This is still what Jesus says to you today: "I am *more* than you imagined."

Jesus wasn't bothered by John's doubts. Still, he warned him, "Blessed is the one who is not offended by me" (Matthew 11:6). If you believe in Jesus despite your doubts, he will exceed your expectations in unbelievable ways. So, doubt your doubts.

Don't Doubt Your Value

Sometimes we doubt God because we doubt ourselves. But John's doubts didn't diminish Jesus's respect for him, nor do yours. Jesus said John was "*more than* a prophet. This is he of whom it is written, 'Behold, I send my messenger before your face, who will prepare your way before you'" (verses 9–10, quoting Malachi 3:1). John was ordained by God and predicted in Scripture.

There's more! Jesus said, "Truly, I say to you, among those born of women there has arisen no one greater than John the Baptist" (Matthew 11:11). Really? The greatest man ever born? Why? Because of his close connection to and his promotion of Jesus. John announced Jesus's coming, baptized him in the Jordan, and sent his own disciples to follow him. That made him greater in God's eyes than Abraham, Moses, or David.

So, what do you suppose Jesus would say about you? We actually know. Verse 11: "The one who is least in the kingdom of heaven is greater than he." Are you a follower of Jesus? Then you are in the kingdom. That makes you greater than John the Baptist. By extension, that makes you greater than Abraham, Moses, and David. How? By your close connection to and your promotion of Jesus.

This is a *lot* to take in! You probably never imagined you were greater than the heroes of the Bible. But it's true! We're greater than the saints of old for two reasons (at least).

First, *we're filled with the Holy Spirit.* Jesus said, "Whoever believes in me, as the Scripture has said, 'Out of his heart will flow rivers of living water.'" John explained, "This he said about the Spirit" (John 7:38–39). As Christians, we have the Spirit of God in us. The Spirit came on the prophets and patriarchs had the Spirit come upon them, but he never stayed long term. He never dwelt *in* individuals until the blood of Jesus atoned for our sins.

Second, *we introduce people to Jesus.* John was great because he announced Jesus's coming; we get to announce Jesus's second coming. John baptized Jesus in the Jordan River; we baptize people into Jesus. John announced Jesus as the Lamb of God; we proclaim him as the risen Savior.

You may be excited to see Moses in heaven. He's *more* excited to see you. You may ask, "What was it like to cross the Red Sea on dry ground?" He'll respond, "Forget the Red Sea. What was it like to lead someone through the waters of baptism?" You may ask King David what it was like when the Spirit came on him, but he'll ask you about the Spirit living inside you. Abraham followed God to the promised land, but you follow Jesus himself. You see, you really are greater because of your connection to and promotion of Jesus.

Key Points

- Everyone has doubts. Even John the Baptist, who was the greatest man besides Jesus.

- Our doubts don't diminish our value to God; he's not offended by them, so make sure you don't stumble over them.

- John was great because of his close connection to and his promotion of Jesus. That's why the least in the kingdom is even greater than John the Baptist.

This Week

❑ **Day 1 (Eyes):** After reading the essay, answer this question: Do you ever doubt your doubts?

❑ **Day 2 (Ears):** There are four servant songs in Isaiah: 42:1–4; 49:1–6; 50:4–9; and 52:13–53:12. What do we learn about Jesus's true nature from them?

❑ **Day 3 (Heart):** Think about how the Holy Spirit in us makes us closer to Jesus: Romans 8:14–17, 2 Corinthians 3:17–18, and Ephesians 1:13.

❑ **Day 4 (Voice):** Discussion:

- What are your greatest doubts about God, Jesus, or the Bible?
- What makes you doubt your doubts?
- How has Jesus been different than you expected but better in the long run?
- How does the Holy Spirit help you personally connect with God? Are there places, practices, or people that help you experience Jesus and his Spirit?

❑ **Day 5 (Hands):** Download the app or go to the website www.roomfordoubt.com.

37

What Makes You a Good Person?

Biblical Concept: Morality
Read: Mark 7:1–23

Different people groups have very different ideas of "clean." For example, in India, you should never shake hands with your left hand. Why? Well, let's just say it's reserved for personal hygiene in a country that often doesn't use toilet paper. In Japan, the idea of carrying around a handkerchief in your pocket is disgusting. They can't understand why the British would want to blow their noses and keep the contents.

In this episode, Jesus got into a heated debate about cultural cleanness. Of all things, it was an argument over handwashing. The stakes were way higher than when Mama says to wash up before supper. This short story may seem silly to some, but it has far-reaching ramifications, as we will see.

A Dinner Party with Baggage

It's at the table, more than any other place, that we set boundaries between insiders and outsiders. And it's nothing new: "When the Pharisees gathered to him, with some of the scribes who had come from Jerusalem, they saw that some of his disciples ate with hands that were defiled, that is, unwashed. (For the Pharisees and all the Jews do not eat unless they wash their hands)" (Mark 7:1–3).

We must understand that these washings were rituals; they weren't for hygiene. Back then people knew nothing of microbes. They weren't washing off dirt; they were washing off cooties. You remember those from recess in the third grade? The Jews believed that the mere touch of an outsider could cause a spiritual infection.

This may sound silly. I assure you, it's not. Every culture, including our own, has rules about whom you can hang around and whom to avoid. These rules may be political, religious, socioeconomic, or racial. All of them, however, are designed to keep your in-group pure from "contamination." Whom we eat with reveals these rules more than anything else. Why? The people you eat with are those you consider fully human.

In the Old Testament, God warned his people about intermarriage with unbelievers (Deuteronomy 7:3). The apostle Paul, of course, gave the same warning: "Do not be unequally yoked with unbelievers. For what partnership has righteousness with lawlessness? Or what fellowship has light with darkness?" (2 Corinthians 6:14).

The rabbis, however, extended the marriage rule to their tables. After all, if you have a foreign guest at your table, your daughter might fall in love, then marry, then reproduce little reprobates. In their minds, this was an extra measure of protection. But it was also another way to identify those who were "in" and those who were "out."

Clean Hands and Dirty Hearts

The Pharisees criticized Jesus's followers for not following their rules: "Why do your disciples not walk according to the tradition of the elders, but eat with defiled hands?" (Mark 7:5). In response, Jesus pointed out that the Pharisees had replaced God's commands with human traditions: "You leave the commandment of God and hold to the tradition of men" (verse 8).

Jesus cited a specific example they couldn't deny (verses 9–13). It's how they used a Jewish rule called Corban. Under this rule, anything devoted to God couldn't be used for any other purpose. So if my parents need a house to live in but I don't want to give them my vacation home, I simply "devote it to God." Now, obviously, *I* can still use it until I die. But I can't give it away. Thus, I use my "religious devotion" to avoid one of the most sacred duties: honoring my father and mother (Deuteronomy 5:16). It's hypocrisy!

Jesus halted the party, called for everyone's attention, and flipped the script. "Hear me, all of you, and understand: There is nothing outside a person that by going into him can defile him, but the things that come out of a person are what defile him" (Mark 7:14–15). The problem isn't unwashed hands; the problem is an unclean heart.

The disciples were confused. When they got him alone, they asked what in the world he meant. His reply wasn't gentle: "Then are you also without understanding? Do you not see that whatever goes into a person from outside cannot defile him, since it enters not his heart but his stomach, and is expelled?" (verses 18–19). Jesus was saying exactly what it sounds like he was saying. Yes, this was potty talk.

As weird as it may sound, this is actually one of the most important things Jesus ever said. Mark explained the impact: "Thus he declared all foods clean" (verse 19). Dietary restrictions (along with Sabbath observance and circumcision) were what identified a good Jew as a good Jew. They identified the insiders.

But Jesus said these regulations were becoming obsolete. Why? Because God now wanted the message of Jesus to go to the ends of the earth—to the outsiders.

These old Jewish laws might seem silly. However, we have our own markers to tell insiders from outsiders. Abstinence from alcohol and certain media, political affiliations, dress. I call it box morality. You get to the center of the box by keeping the rules. The most righteous are at the center of the box. In this encounter, however, Jesus destroyed the box. Jesus transformed ethics. It's no longer about getting to the center of the box to avoid unclean outsiders. It's about moving out of the box toward outsiders.

To quote Jesus, "What comes out of a person is what defiles him. For from within, out of the heart of man, come evil thoughts, sexual immorality, theft, murder, adultery, coveting, wickedness, deceit, sensuality, envy, slander, pride, foolishness. All these evil things come from within, and they defile a person" (verses 20–23). If the church is to go global and accept people from all walks of life, having the right heart is more important than keeping "right" rules.

Key Points

- Meals are socially and spiritually significant.
- Dietary restrictions are now obsolete because God wants the gospel to go to the whole world.
- Jesus declared all foods clean. This shifted morality from external rules to the motives of a person's heart.

This Week

❑ **Day 1 (Eyes):** After reading the essay, answer this question: What do you do to signal to others you are a good Christian?

❑ **Day 2 (Ears):** How does Isaiah 58 answer the question, "What makes you a good person?"

❑ **Day 3 (Heart):** Think about how these principles could apply to other areas of your life: Acts 15:20, Romans 14:14, and 1 Corinthians 8:7.

❑ **Day 4 (Voice):** Discussion:

- Share about your favorite meal—not what you like to eat but a memory you made at a specific place and time.
- Why are meals so important for building relationships with people?
- Does your church have many external rules—ways to signal your righteousness? What are they?
- How could you use meals to open the door to a relationship with someone far from God?

❑ **Day 5 (Hands):** Schedule a meal with one of your friends whom you don't know well and who doesn't know Jesus well.

38

Who Do You Say Jesus Is?

Biblical Concept: Declaration
Read: Matthew 16:13–28

Every relationship must have the DTR talk—to define the relationship. Are we just friends, or are we really committed to each other? This conversation happens in romantic relationships, friendships, and even your relationship with God. Two years into his ministry, Jesus had the DTR with his apostles. At some point, he'll have that conversation with you. Perhaps he already has. How you answer will determine more than you can imagine.

A Distant Place for a Close Conversation

Jesus wanted to have this important conversation in just the right place. He chose Caesarea Philippi, twenty-five miles north of Capernaum. The place itself implied the importance of the question.

In the days of King David, this area was known as Dan. It was the northernmost city of the kingdom. After David, the nation split. To make matters worse, the leader of the new northern kingdom set up a golden calf in Dan. Some thought this was okay. The prophets, however, called it what it was—idolatry.

Dan represented the moment when Israel was broken and began to recognize their need for a Messiah. That made Dan the perfect place for this DTR. So Jesus asked, "Who do people say that the Son of Man is?" (Matthew 16:13).

The answers offered were John the Baptist, Elijah, Jeremiah, or one of the other prophets. I'm sure the apostles thought this was a compliment. However, to equate Jesus with even these greats is to damn him with faint praise. He is far more than a powerful prophet.

The Most Important Question You'll Ever Be Asked

Jesus had already heard all the gossip. He focused the question: "Who do *you* say that I am?" (verse 15). That's what really mattered, and it matters just as much for us. At some point, we will all have to answer, whether here or in eternity.

Peter spoke for the group: "You are the Christ, the Son of the living God" (verse 16). That's huge. Jesus was the long-awaited Messiah. In their minds, that meant Jesus was to be the king of Israel—a warrior who would brutally destroy all enemies of the state. That was Peter's expectation (and hope). Jesus was about to shatter it.

To begin, though, Jesus affirmed Peter: "Blessed are you, Simon Bar-Jonah! For flesh and blood has not revealed this to you, but my Father who is in heaven. And I tell you, you are Peter, and on this rock I will build my church, and the gates of hell shall not prevail against it. I will give you the keys of the kingdom of heaven" (verses 17–19).

Three words require a bit of explanation. First, Peter is the rock on which the church is built. It's a clever play on words since *Peter* actually means "rock." There's some debate as to whether Peter himself is the rock or whether his confession is the foundation of the church. Whatever this might mean, however, Jesus is building a church!

Second, *church* (*ekklēsia*) means "those called to an assembly." It's a Greek word used for a public gathering (Acts 19:32). When God calls the assembly, it becomes sacred. The *ekklēsia* is a spiritual kingdom, not an ethnic group, social club, or political party.

Finally, the keys Jesus gave Peter represent the authority to lock or unlock the door of salvation. As a believer, you share that authority and responsibility to preach Jesus and announce his forgiveness to those who repent and make him Lord (2 Corinthians 5:20).

Jesus is building his church. He said, "The gates of hell shall not prevail against it" (Matthew 16:18). He ensures its ultimate victory—just not how the disciples had imagined.

I'm Not Who You Think

As soon as Peter made his confession, Jesus course corrected: "From that time Jesus began to show his disciples that he must go to Jerusalem and suffer many things from the elders and chief priests and scribes, and be killed, and on the third day be raised" (verse 21). He identified the specific place he would be killed and the people who would kill him. How did the disciples miss it?

A victorious king *and* a suffering servant seemed contradictory. Peter said, "Far be it from you, Lord! This shall never happen to you" (verse 22). Let that sink in—Peter *rebuked* Jesus. That wasn't going to go well. Jesus rebuked Peter in return: "Get behind me, Satan! You are a hindrance to me. For you are not setting your mind on the things of God, but on the things of man" (verse 23). Oh snap! He just called Peter "Satan" (which means "adversary"). It may seem harsh, but it's not inaccurate. Peter was tempting Jesus to avoid the cross. That was the very thing the devil tried to do during Jesus's wilderness temptations (Matthew 4:8–10).

Jesus then turned to the other apostles (and to us!) and gave this crucial command. It is, in fact, the most frequently cited saying of Jesus. We shouldn't disregard it. "If anyone would come after me, let him deny himself and take up his cross and follow me. For whoever would save his life will lose it, but whoever loses his life for my sake will find it" (Matthew 16:24–25).

One-third of all cross talk in the Gospels is about the cross *we take up* in following Jesus. Hence, the cross is not just Jesus's sacrifice but ours as well. When Jesus died on the cross, he saved the world from her sins. When we die on the cross, we save society from hers. Through selfless love and service, we can bring healing to communities. Not only is the cross Jesus's path to victory; it's ours too. If we lay down our lives, God will raise us up.

Key Points

- This is the most important question you'll ever be asked: "Who do you say Jesus is?"

- Jesus had to suffer as a servant before reigning as a king.

- The cross of Jesus saves the world from her sins; the cross of Christians saves society from her sins.

This Week

- ☐ **Day 1 (Eyes):** After reading the essay, who do you say Jesus is?

- ☐ **Day 2 (Ears):** Read the story of Rehoboam and Jeroboam in 1 Kings 12. How might Jesus think about his own royal career in light of this history?

- ☐ **Day 3 (Heart):** Think about 2 Corinthians 4:10–12, Galatians 2:20, and Philippians 3:10–11. What do these verses say about being crucified with Christ?

- ☐ **Day 4 (Voice):** Discussion:
  - Share how you came to faith in Jesus. Was it through a process or a crisis (or both)?
  - What's the difference between believing in Jesus as Lord and believing in him as Savior? Can you really do one without the other?
  - In what ways do you think the church has misunderstood or misrepresented Jesus's true identity?
  - How is it that Christians taking up their crosses leads to salvation for society? Can you offer an example of how that works?

- ☐ **Day 5 (Hands):** Think carefully about how to answer this question: Who do you say Jesus is? Write your answer in a single sentence. Now find someone to share that with this week.

39

What's Worth
Worrying About?

Biblical Concept: Anxiety
Read: Luke 10:38–42

Anxiety disorders have increased 1,200 percent in the last four decades.[1] They have now passed depression and all other disorders as the most common mental illness in America.[2] Some professionals estimate that one of every three adults suffers from an anxiety disorder. That counts as a pandemic.

Some people with anxiety disorders will require counseling or medical treatment. If that's you, please seek the help you need to be healthy. At the same time, we should recognize that all mental health disorders have at their root a spiritual component. Therefore, faith in Jesus Christ should be at the core of any treatment for mental health issues. Jesus is the great physician whose wisdom and power can heal our bodies, souls, and minds. Let's take a look at one example from the life of Jesus.

Two Sisters

Mary and Martha were sisters. Their brother, Lazarus, was one of Jesus's best friends. They lived two miles from Jerusalem, just over the Mount of

Olives, so we meet them in the Gospels from time to time when Jesus was in the area. In fact, the entire chapter of John 11 is dedicated to the story of Lazarus's resurrection. The sisters, of course, were there and played a crucial role. They were the ones who sent a message to Jesus begging him to come heal Lazarus before he died.

About a year before Jesus raised Lazarus, Mary and Martha had invited him to dinner. It would be a nice retreat since Jesus was under quite a bit of pressure at the time. Undoubtedly, they fussed over menus, recipes, and seating arrangements. After their extensive preparations, shopping, and sweat equity in the kitchen, Jesus arrived with the boys. All was set for a memorable event, which it was, but not for the reasons Martha had imagined.

Martha executed her plan to perfection. Mary, on the other hand, got swept up in Jesus's teaching. She sat at his feet, giving him undivided attention. Martha worked double-time to make sure the banquet went off without a hitch. With every dish she served, her anger increased. Martha was doing everything she could to be a Martha Stewart, but her sister was literally sitting down on the job! To make matters worse, never had a rabbi allowed a woman to sit as a student. Jesus was simply ignoring this irresponsible behavior. Mary was *out of line,* and Jesus was letting her get away with it!

Martha was beside herself, while Mary was beside Jesus. Finally Martha snapped, asking Jesus to order Mary back into the kitchen: "Lord, do you not care that my sister has left me to serve alone?" (Luke 10:40). The word translated "left" literally means "abandoned," which is quite dramatic. Jesus's answer points the way to higher priorities: "Martha, Martha, you are anxious and troubled about many things, but one thing is necessary. Mary has chosen the good portion, which will not be taken away from her" (verses 41–42).

Why We Worry

Well, how do you like that? Jesus simply told Martha, "Don't worry." Rather than worrying about little things, we need to start focusing on the one thing that *really* matters. He was right; there's only one thing necessary, and it's Jesus himself. Mary actually had her priorities straight. Martha was incredibly fortunate to have Jesus in her home. But she missed the moment. What about you? If Jesus showed up at your house right now, would you worry about the dishes? Honestly, some would.

So why do we worry? Two reasons really: (1) physical needs and (2) social approval. That may sound like an oversimplification, but it really isn't. Matthew 6 deals head on with both concerns (see chapters 29 and 30). In the second half of Matthew 6, Jesus tells us to trust in God's provision. He feeds the birds and clothes the flowers, and he cares even more about his children. In the first half of the chapter, Jesus tells us to seek approval from God alone. He is our Father. He sees in secret and rewards us. That's a lesson Martha missed. How about you?

Personal aside: virtually every time I experience anxiety, it's because I fear someone's disapproval. When I get an aggressive email or miss an appointment or deadline, my mind shifts into overdrive. I script out my defensive response, my justifications and rebuttals. Why? Because I don't fully believe God has my back. Even while typing this, I'm embarrassed about how small my faith is. Like Martha, I'm trying to manipulate God's opinion of me rather than experiencing the love God has for me.

Jesus told Martha (and us) not to worry. God our Father has *already promised* to take care of us. He'll give you what you need. He's also *already promised* to give us the approval we seek. He's got your back! If we search for provision or approval anywhere else, it will always lead to worry.

Paul offered an effective solution to worry: "Do not be anxious about anything, but in everything by prayer and supplication with thanksgiving let your requests be made known to God" (Philippians 4:6). Is it really possible to remove all anxiety? No, of course not. But we can reduce it

significantly. The story of Martha tells us how: *get your priorities right.*
How do we do that? According to Philippians 4:6, it's through *prayers of*
thanksgiving. When we thank God for all he's done for us, we're reminded
of his meticulous care for us. That's the secret to a worry-free life.

Key Points

- Martha was worried about impressing Jesus. Mary chose to be impressed by Jesus.

- The solution to worry is prioritizing Jesus.

- Prayers of thanksgiving set your priorities right.

This Week

❏ **Day 1 (Eyes):** After reading the essay, answer this question: Do you have the right priorities to minimize worry in your life?

❏ **Day 2 (Ears):** Read Psalm 37. Underline each verse that speaks to your present situation.

❏ **Day 3 (Heart):** Think about Philippians 4:6. Take time to actually memorize it with this video: https://core52.org/week/week-48.[3]

❏ **Day 4 (Voice):** Discussion:

- Make a list of things you're worrying about, perhaps on a whiteboard (or a window in your home with erasable markers). Now put them in two columns: social approval and physical needs.
- As an anti-anxiety exercise, make a list of things you're grateful to God for.
- Is your worry in your head or in your body? True anxiety disorders have physical manifestations such as shortness of breath, insomnia, extreme fatigue, and/or heart palpitations. If you have anxiety in your body, share that with your parent or guardian so you can get the appropriate help.
- Worst-case scenario exercise: Take one item on your list. Play it out to the ultimate extreme. What's the worst thing that could happen? How do the scriptures in the New Testament address this worst-case scenario?

❏ **Day 5 (Hands):** Recite Philippians 4:6. Now do it.

Section 4

The Passion of Jesus

Leading up to the Cross, we want to look at Jesus's **preparation** for his death. We'll then look at the **suffering** itself, both spiritually and physically. This takes us beyond the grave to Jesus's **victory** in the Resurrection and Ascension, which point to his ultimate return when our quest will finally end in eternity.

> **Preparation:** chapters 40–43
> **Suffering:** chapters 44–48
> **Victory:** chapters 49–52

40

Was Jesus Political?
Part I

Biblical Concept: Politics
Read: Luke 19:29–44

Politics seems so messy and divisive. So to ask whether Jesus was political may seem awkward, but it actually is an important question. Let's start with a definition. The word *political* comes from the same Greek root as *politeuomai,* meaning "to live as a citizen" (Philippians 1:27). Politics is about forming a community. Therefore, a political figure must (1) be public, not private, (2) have an identifiable group of followers, (3) have a social agenda, and (4) exercise power over people.

Did Jesus fit the description? Absolutely. However, while politicians are known for using power to promote and protect themselves, Jesus used power only for the powerless. His brand of being political overturned traditional politics.

Jesus Claimed to Be King

Although Jesus never verbally claimed to be king (which would have been suicide), his actions spoke louder than words. His selection of twelve apostles showed his intention of restoring the twelve tribes of Israel. His commissioning of seventy-two evangelists (Luke 10:1) mirrored the seventy-one members of the Sanhedrin (the Jewish Supreme Court). He compared himself to Moses, who founded the nation, as well as David, her premier king. He claimed to be a shepherd, a judge, and the Messiah—all important leadership roles.

One incident, however, was more obviously political than any other. The Triumphal Entry was straight-up political theater. It's so important that all four Gospels record it.

It began in a suburb of Jerusalem known as Bethphage. Jesus sent two of his men to go get a colt. "As they were untying the colt, its owners said to them, 'Why are you untying the colt?' And they said, 'The Lord has need of it'" (Luke 19:33–34). We can only guess that the owners knew Jesus. It's possible he had healed one of their relatives during one of his frequent speaking engagements in the area. But wait. A colt? Why did Jesus want a colt?

Matthew identified the moment as a fulfillment of prophecy: "'Behold, your king is coming to you, humble, and mounted on a donkey, on a colt, the foal of a beast of burden'" (21:5, quoting Zechariah 9:9). Zechariah prophesied that the new king—the Messiah—would come on a colt. The remainder of Zechariah's book is filled with messianic prophecy:

- **The thirty pieces of silver** Judas Iscariot was paid to betray Jesus: "I took *the thirty pieces of silver* and threw them into the house of the LORD" (Zechariah 11:13, fulfilled in Matthew 27:9–10).

- **Jesus pierced at his crucifixion:** "When they look on me, on *him whom they have pierced,* they shall mourn for him, as one mourns for an only child, and weep bitterly over him, as one weeps over a firstborn" (Zechariah 12:10, fulfilled in John 19:34, 37).

- **Strike the shepherd,** and the sheep will scatter: *"Strike the shepherd,* and the sheep will be scattered; I will turn my hand against the little ones" (Zechariah 13:7, fulfilled in Matthew 26:31; Mark 14:27).

- **The Mount of Olives** and the appearance of the Messiah: "On that day his feet shall stand on *the Mount of Olives* that lies before Jerusalem on the east" (Zechariah 14:4). This happens to be the exact spot of the Triumphal Entry.

Clearly, there's more here than meets the Western eye. The timing of Passover, the location of the Mount of Olives, and the colt on which Jesus rode were all clear signs that he was claiming to be king. However, Jesus used his power only for the powerless. So began a brand-new kind of politics.

The Crowds Affirmed Jesus as King

Jesus's intentions couldn't have been clearer. The crowd's approval was equally clear. We may not see it through the lens of our own culture. But if you put on the lens of the Middle East, their actions shouted their praise of their new king:

- The disciples spread their cloaks on the colt for Jesus to sit on (Luke 19:35).

- The crowds spread their cloaks on the road for the donkey to walk on (Matthew 21:8; 2 Kings 9:13).

- They cut palm branches and waved them and laid them on the ground as a red carpet (Mark 11:8; John 12:13). Waving palm branches was a sign that royalty was in the room (Revelation 7:9).

- They started singing Psalm 118:25–26: "Hosanna [which means 'save now!'] to the Son of David!" (Matthew 21:9). This was a clear reference to the messianic king.

It was a magnificent moment. That's why what happened next was so unexpected. Jesus wept over the city. He didn't just shed a tear; the word Luke used indicates deep, audible sobs: "Would that you, even you, had known on this day the things that make for peace! But now they are hidden from your eyes" (Luke 19:42).

In a moment when most politicians would soak in the praise, Jesus wept for his people. He knew full well that his coronation would be with a crown of thorns. He knew that a terrible price would be paid for rejecting him. Yet he walked straight into the teeth of suffering and death, knowing the power of the Resurrection.

This sets a new gold standard for leadership. A leader's goal is no longer popularity and power. Rather, leadership is measured by service and sacrifice. The endgame of leadership is not power but a legacy of love. Jesus was political for sure. But he redefined the purpose of politics. As his followers, subjects, and servants, our promotion of our king should reflect his political practice of using power only for the powerless. By this we will win the world and make Jesus famous.

Key Points

- Jesus doesn't appear political to us because we're used to politicians using power for self-promotion and self-protection. Jesus used power only for the powerless.

- Though Jesus never verbally claimed a political title, his actions clearly indicated his intent to be the king of Israel.

- The Triumphal Entry was the most politically charged event of his career. He clearly claimed to be king, and the crowds publicly declared their support.

This Week

☐ **Day 1 (Eyes):** After reading the essay, answer this question: What difference would it make to you if Jesus really were the president of the world, not just the Savior of your soul?

☐ **Day 2 (Ears):** Psalm 118 was quoted by the crowds at the Triumphal Entry. What other verses in this poem reflect the life of Jesus?

☐ **Day 3 (Heart):** Think about Acts 17:7, 1 Corinthians 15:24–25, and Revelation 11:15. How do these verses portray Jesus as a political figure?

☐ **Day 4 (Voice):** Discussion:

- Had you ever thought of Jesus as a political figure? Does that resonate with you or seem unsettling? Why?
- If Jesus were president, what do you think his policies would look like?
- What's the difference between living as if Jesus is your Savior and living as if he is your king?
- If you were campaigning for Jesus, what would your strategy be to make him famous?

☐ **Day 5 (Hands):** Pull out one item from your campaign strategy this week and put it into practice.

41

Was Jesus Political?
Part 2

Biblical Concept: Authority
Read: Mark 11:12–25

When I'm hungry (or hangry), I'm not a nice person. If I have to wait more than an hour for dinner, I get all kinds of cranky. It's sad, but it helps me appreciate one of the weirdest moments in Jesus's ministry. He cursed a fig tree for not providing breakfast. His motives were better than mine. So there has got to be more to the story than meets the eye. There is—a *lot* more.

A Fit over Figs

The final Sunday before the Crucifixion, Jesus had ridden down the Mount of Olives in what is now known as the Triumphal Entry. He proclaimed himself as the King of the Jews. When the dust settled, the disciples returned to Bethany, where they were staying during Passover.

"On the following day [Monday], when they came from Bethany, [Jesus] was hungry. And seeing in the distance a fig tree in leaf, he went to see if he could find anything on it. When he came to it, he found nothing but leaves, for it was not the season for figs. And he said to it, 'May no one ever eat fruit from you again' " (Mark 11:12–14). That seems rather rude to the unsuspecting fig tree. Perhaps a bit of background would make more sense of this.

With the Triumphal Entry the day before, it's reasonable to assume that Jesus might have missed supper as he often did when he got too busy (Mark 3:20; 6:31). It was only April, so all he could hope for were *unripe* figs. They would be bitter but edible. The fact that there were none meant there wouldn't be any in the future. This fig tree was fruitless.

Mark shaped the story in a way that makes it hard to miss the message. He told about the cursing of the fig tree, followed by the cleansing of the temple. He then circled back to the fig tree. Mark was making a literary sandwich. The incident in the middle is the meat, flavoring the bread on either side. Bottom line: Jesus's action against the fig tree is a prophetic parable, parallel to the cleansing of the temple. Both show the destiny of a fruitless nation because of their rejection of their Messiah.

The "Cleansing" of the Temple

This title in our Bibles is a bit misleading. Jesus didn't exactly cleanse the temple. Rather, he threatened it: "He entered the temple and began to drive out those who sold and those who bought in the temple, and he overturned the tables of the money-changers and the seats of those who sold pigeons. And he would not allow anyone to carry anything through the temple" (Mark 11:15–16). Why would he do that?

Again, a bit of background will help. Annas, the high priest, had set up a crooked system to make money from pilgrims' sacrifices. Specifically, the sacrificial lambs were sold at inflated prices. If you brought your own lamb, some priests were tasked with making sure it was worthy. It wouldn't pass inspection, of course. You would be forced to buy a worthy lamb at an outrageous price! Furthermore, the priests would accept payment only in the temple shekel, which could be obtained from the money changers—with an exchange fee, of course.

Jesus explained his motive: "Is it not written, 'My house shall be called a house of prayer for all the nations'? But you have made it a den of robbers" (verse 17). This is actually a quote combining Isaiah 56:7 and Jeremiah 7:11. Both texts were carefully chosen, and together they send a powerful and threatening message.

Isaiah 56 looks forward to a day when everyone who believes in the Messiah—even outsiders—will have equal standing before God, even in the temple. But the chief priests had set up their market in the only part of the temple where outsiders were allowed, making it hard for them to worship. This was *not* okay with Jesus.

Jeremiah 7:4 says, "Do not trust in these deceptive words: 'This is the temple of the LORD, the temple of the LORD, the temple of the LORD.'" The people believed that they were safe from judgment because they maintained the temple for God. Jeremiah warned that God *would* destroy the temple if their worship was false. In 586 BC, God did.

Taken in context, Jesus's quotation was a stern warning: repent or repeat your history. History did, in fact, repeat. That temple was destroyed in AD 70 and has never been rebuilt. It has, however, been replaced with the spiritual temple—the body of Christ (1 Corinthians 6:16–19; 2 Corinthians 6:16; Ephesian 2:19–22; 1 Peter 2:5).

This reminds us of an earlier incident. At the beginning of his ministry, Jesus also cleared the temple courts. Thus, threatening the temple bracketed his ministry. Back then he told us exactly what he was up to: "Destroy this temple, and in three days I will raise it up" (John 2:19).

Jesus's body is the new temple. That's why his resurrection launched a new era of the temple. All nations can now enter and be included in his new body. In this renewed kingdom, citizenship is open to every tongue, tribe, and nation. That kingdom of God is the temple of Christ, where true worship and sacrifice are performed. This is the epicenter of the politics of Jesus. A new nation of people whose citizenship is in heaven even as we spread his fame to every corner of the earth.

Key Points

- The cursing of the fig tree is an enacted parable predicting the destruction of the temple.

- Jesus quoted from Isaiah 56 and Jeremiah 7, threatening the temple because the nation was fruitless like the barren fig tree.

- Jesus himself is the temple. It was destroyed and raised up again in three days, launching a new era of a global temple we call the body of Christ or the church. This defines the politics of Jesus.

This Week

☐ **Day 1 (Eyes):** After reading the essay, how would you describe Jesus's political agenda?

☐ **Day 2 (Ears):** Read Isaiah 56:1–8 and Jeremiah 7:1–11. How does this context help you see more fully what Jesus was up to?

☐ **Day 3 (Heart):** Think about 1 Corinthians 6:16–19, 2 Corinthians 6:16, and Ephesians 2:19–22. What do these verses say about Jesus's politics?

☐ **Day 4 (Voice):** Discussion:

- What's the difference between cleansing the temple and threatening the temple?
- We often hear, "Your body is the temple of God," meaning your own physical body. How would it change your view if you read *body* as "the church"? (See the verses in day 3.)
- After reading Isaiah 56:1–8 and Jeremiah 7:1–11, answer these questions: How does your church align with the social priorities of Jesus? How do you personally align?
- What social concerns would be part of Jesus's political agenda? Lean into Isaiah 56 and Jeremiah 7 for your answers.

☐ **Day 5 (Hands):** Take up one item from Jesus's political agenda, and develop an action plan for carrying it out where you live, work, or play.

42

Was Jesus Full of Himself?

Biblical Concept: Humility
Read: John 13:1–20

Can I confess something to you? I'm not a particularly humble person. Now you might think, *Well, that's because you're preaching at a large church, you write books, and you have a social media following.* Nope. My "confidence" doesn't come from public accomplishments. It comes more from my private insecurities. I'm constantly tempted to present myself as more than I am because I fear I'll be found out to be less than others imagine.

Perhaps that's why this chapter and the next are so important to me. Jesus had an incredibly high view of himself. He said things like "I am the light of the world, the judge of the earth. Without me, you can do nothing. I am the Son of God!" (Matthew 25:31–32; John 8:12; 10:36; 15:5). Yet none can equal his service to the least and the lost. It seems like a contradiction, but it's not. Here's why: *in the Bible, humility is not how you feel about yourself but how you treat others.* No incident proves that more than Jesus washing his apostles' feet.

Setting the Table

Jesus was well aware that this was his Last Supper: "Jesus knew that his hour had come to depart out of this world to the Father, [and] having loved his own who were in the world, he loved them to the end" (John 13:1). Within twenty-four hours, Peter would deny him, Judas would betray him, the chief priests would condemn him, and the Romans would crucify him. Jesus predicted each detail.

Jesus was brooding; the Twelve were tense. Something was wrong. John lets his readers in on the secret: "The devil had already put it into the heart of Judas Iscariot, Simon's son, to betray him" (verse 2). There was a traitor at the table. Think about that. Jesus knew the Cross was coming, he knew Peter would deny him, and he knew Judas would betray him. Jesus demonstrated humility when it was least convenient.

Washing of Feet

Because people back then walked on dusty roads in sandals, it was normal to wash your feet before a banquet. You never wanted to dirty your host's expensive carpets. This wasn't the kind of job *anyone* enjoyed. It wasn't primarily the smell of the feet that was the problem; ancient cities had bad smells everywhere! Rather, in a shame-honor culture, it was dishonorable to touch feet. That's why the task was given to the lowest servant in the house.

It comes as no surprise that none of the Twelve volunteered for the job. Since they believed Jesus was about to be inaugurated, they were posturing for political positions in the soon-coming kingdom. Jesus volunteered. You could have heard a pin drop when he disrobed down to his loincloth. This made him appear as a slave (John 19:23–24; Philippians 2:7).

Jesus washed twenty-four feet right in a row. All his disciples—even Judas. Just think about that! Jesus had read the prophecies about Judas (Psalm 41:9; 69:25; 109:8; Zechariah 11:12; Acts 1:20). He knew Judas was about to betray him—that very night. Yet he still washed Judas's feet in one last attempt to recover him. If that's what Jesus did for Judas, imagine the patience he has with you. Don't underestimate how far Jesus will go to recover you as his disciple.

The Lesson of the Basin and Towel

The basin and towel would be replaced by a cross the very next day. If that's how Jesus lived and died, then we, his followers, must follow suit. Jesus is calling us to a lifestyle of service, not a single act. Here's how he explained it:

> If I then, your Lord and Teacher, have washed your feet, you also ought to wash one another's feet. For I have given you an example, that you also should do just as I have done to you. Truly, truly, I say to you, a servant is not greater than his master, nor is a messenger greater than the one who sent him. If you know these things, blessed are you if you do them. (John 13:14–17)

The practice of washing feet is foreign to us today. However, the humble service it represented has never been more needed. It's the constant call for a Christian classmate, neighbor, teammate, and friend. There are unlimited expressions of humble service, but none of us are exempt if we call Jesus Lord. Simple, right? Not so fast. What happened next shows us how difficult it is to humble ourselves to serve others.

The Debate at the Table

In the middle of this meal, the apostles argued about which one of them was the greatest (Luke 22:24). They'd had the same argument a year earlier (Matthew 18:1–5; Mark 9:33–37; Luke 9:46–48) and again just a week earlier (Matthew 20:20–28; Mark 10:35–45). That total lack of self-awareness seems unbelievable! But we're often no different.

After Jesus washed their feet, they argued about who should sit closest to him. (The seating arrangement showed who was most important.) They were elbowing for positions of power when Jesus became king. But they missed the fact that his crown would be a crown of thorns.

As I apply this lesson to my own life and my own struggle with humility, I realize that my quest for position and power is usually due not to arrogance but to insecurity. Only those confident in their relationship with God can fully embrace humble service. For many of us, humility is threatening to our fragile self-esteem. The solution is to fully embrace the love of God through Jesus Christ. When we grasp *whose* we are, we know *who* we are. Then we can serve others without worrying about our status.

Key Points

- Washing feet was a sign of humble service. It foreshadowed the Cross, which was humble sacrifice in death.

- If we claim to follow Jesus, we must also imitate his actions.

- The disciples' argument about who was the greatest shows just how difficult this lesson is to apply in real time.

This Week

❏ **Day 1 (Eyes):** After reading the essay, answer this question: Do you have confidence in who you are before God?

❏ **Day 2 (Ears):** Read Daniel 4. Contrast this story of King Nebuchadnezzar with the story of Jesus.

❏ **Day 3 (Heart):** Think about Romans 7:6, 2 Corinthians 4:5, and Galatians 5:13. Can you be humble without self-sacrifice?

❏ **Day 4 (Voice):** Discussion:

- What is your least favorite household chore?
- Do you tend to think of humility as your attitude about yourself or your actions toward others? What difference does that make in how you define humility?
- Make a list of actions that would be equivalent in our culture to foot washing in Jesus's day.
- Do you find doing these kinds of things easy or hard? Why?

❏ **Day 5 (Hands):** Identify and do one act of humble service for someone you live with. Don't say anything to anyone about what you've done.

43

What Did Jesus Think About Himself?

Biblical Concept: Sacrament
Read: Mark 14:1–25

One year I was in Jerusalem at a tattoo shop with my two best friends. The family who owns the shop has been doing tattoos for *seven hundred years.* My friends looked at me and asked, "Are you ready to get a tattoo?" And that's how it happened. The cross on my calf is a symbol of my love for God and for my friends that share this mark of faith. It's cool, but it's just a symbol, like a flag or a wedding ring. A sacrament? Well, that's a whole other level. Not only do sacraments represent something; they also reflect divine realities. In the church, we have two sacraments: baptism and the Lord's Supper. Power beyond the elements connects us to God in ways our eyes can't see. That's why the Lord's Supper has been so important to virtually every church in every country for the entirety of church history.

Preparations for Passover

Jesus was on a collision course with the cross. From the eyewitnesses' perspective, it must have seemed like a derailed freight train rushing toward a cliff. From God's bird's-eye view, it was a carefully orchestrated symphony.

Preparation by enemies. Two days before Passover, the Sanhedrin (the Jewish Supreme Court) had an emergency meeting. They wanted to get rid of Jesus, but he was wildly popular. If they grabbed him from the temple, they risked a riot. They were stuck. That is, until Judas showed up on their doorstep, offering to hand over the Master. We may never know Judas's motives. But one thing seems clear: God's sovereign design was at work (John 17:12), as well as satanic possession (Luke 22:3; John 13:27) and Judas's own greed.

Preparation by friends. Five days earlier, Mary, in stark contrast to Judas, anointed Jesus's feet with valuable ointment. It was worth about a year's wages! The apostles, led by Judas (John 12:4–5), objected. They accused her of wasting funds that could have been used to feed the poor. Jesus came to her defense: "Leave her alone. Why do you trouble her? She has done a beautiful thing to me. . . . She has anointed my body beforehand for burial" (Mark 14:6, 8). She saw that Jesus was about to die and anointed him for burial while she had the chance. She was the only one who listened and responded to Jesus's predictions of his death.

Preparation by Jesus. "On the first day of Unleavened Bread, when they sacrificed the Passover lamb, his disciples said to him, "Where will you have us go and prepare for you to eat the Passover?" (verse 12). Jesus knew there was a warrant out for his arrest. So he told the disciples the plan: find the house by following a man carrying a jar of water (which men typically wouldn't do). This looks like a prearranged secret meeting place; everything was already set up (verses 12–17).

The table was arranged with U-shaped seating. The host reclined at the head of the U. The chief seats were directly behind Jesus (Judas) and in front of him (John). The conversation began like a shot from a cannon: "Truly, I say to you, one of you will betray me, one who is eating with me" (verse 18). A bit later, John leaned back against Jesus's chest and asked, "Who is it?" In a conversation only John and Judas could hear, Jesus said, " 'It is he to whom I will give this morsel of bread when I have dipped it.' So when he had dipped the morsel, he gave it to Judas, the son of Simon Iscariot" (John 13:25–26). Now John knew, but it was too late to stop him. Judas ran into the night.

The Fulfillment of Passover

Passover is the most important Jewish holiday. This seven-day celebration culminates in a meal where each item on the table tells part of the story of how Israel became a nation. Every detail points to Jesus. The table is telling *his* story, not simply history. Two elements are particularly important: the bread and the wine.

The unleavened bread is a reminder of the haste with which the Israelites fled captivity in Egypt. There was no time for the bread to rise with leaven. Since leaven sometimes represents sin, the unleavened bread signifies sinlessness. Jesus is the sinless one through whose suffering we find freedom. That's why "as they were eating, he took bread, and after blessing it broke it and gave it to them, and said, 'Take; this is my body' " (Mark 14:22). The bread represents his body on the cross, torn to release us from slavery to sin. This was the institution of the Lord's Supper, or communion.

"He took a cup, and when he had given thanks he gave it to them, saying, 'Drink of it, all of you, for this is my blood of the covenant, which is poured out for many for the forgiveness of sins' " (Matthew 26:27–28). The wine represents Jesus's blood, shed for our forgiveness—the fulfillment of the Passover lamb. The Exodus from Egypt was only a foreshadowing of our ultimate release from slavery to sin.

This miniature meal contains a world of meaning. It represents our new covenant, promised back in the days of Jeremiah (31:31–34). In the new covenant, you no longer make a sacrifice for God; rather, he offered a sacrifice for you (Isaiah 53:12; Mark 10:45; John 1:29). With this meal,

Jesus showed what he thought of himself. He claimed to be the Passover lamb. He believed he was Moses, leading the nation to spiritual freedom. He was the sinless offering, and his blood was the new covenant between God and human beings. When we receive the elements of communion, we also affirm a depth of history embodied in him.

Key Points

- God carefully orchestrated the events surrounding the Lord's Supper.

- Passover told the story of Israel's beginning; it was ultimately fulfilled by Jesus.

- The Lord's Supper is a sacrament through which we celebrate and connect with the sacrifice of Jesus.

This Week

❏ **Day 1 (Eyes):** After reading the essay, answer this question: How did Jesus view himself?

❏ **Day 2 (Ears):** Read the story of the Passover in Exodus 12. How do you see the life of Jesus reflected in this story?

❏ **Day 3 (Heart):** Think about 1 Corinthians 5:7, 1 Peter 1:19, and Revelation 5:12. What do these verses say about Jesus as the lamb?

❏ **Day 4 (Voice):** Discussion:

- Can you give an example of how history repeats itself?
- What's the difference between a symbol and a sacrament? Feel free to use Google for some basic definitions. Can you give examples of each?
- Go to www.biblegateway.com. Type in the word *lamb*. Find out which New Testament book contains the most uses of that word, and read each verse.
- Share why the Lord's Supper is meaningful to you. What could you do to make it more meaningful?

❏ **Day 5 (Hands):** Prepare a meal with family and/or friends. Celebrate communion at that meal.

44

How Can I Survive Difficult Days?

Biblical Concept: Hope
Read: John 14:1–31

I was living overseas when I got some earth-shattering news. It could have changed my life trajectory and definitely would damage a relationship dear to me. It was my dark night of the soul. Overwhelmed and alone, I called my best friend in Texas. He listened intently. When I was done, he said, "Do you need me to come?" He was ready to put his life on pause and fly halfway around the world to be with me. That day, I learned that presence is more important than solutions. That's Jesus's promise to you.

Let's eavesdrop on a conversation Jesus had with his disciples the night before he died. John 14 begins and ends with an identical line: "Let not your hearts be troubled" (verses 1, 27). Jesus prepared his disciples with three promises that would sustain them through difficult days. They will sustain you as well.

1. The Promise of a Place with the Father

"Let not your hearts be troubled. Believe in God; believe also in me. In my Father's house are many rooms. If it were not so, would I have told you that I go to prepare a place for you? And if I go and prepare a place for you, I will come again and will take you to myself, that where I am you may be also. And you know the way to where I am going" (verses 1–4). What a great promise!

The place Jesus is preparing is not a physical house but a place in the Father's family. He's making a space for us with the Father's heart. How? In this very moment, he sits at the Father's right hand, pleading your case (Romans 8:34). Because of Jesus's nail-scarred hands, the Father's verdict is "not guilty."

Don't miss this. Jesus used the term *Father* twenty-three times in this passage! Because of Jesus's death, resurrection, and ascension, God is now our Father. We're no longer just his creation; we're also his children. He stands between us and our enemies. He will never leave us or forsake us!

Like most of us, Thomas missed it: "Lord, we do not know where you are going. How can we know the way?" (verse 5). He, too, was thinking about a place rather than a position. Jesus clarified: "I am the way, and the truth, and the life. No one comes to the Father except through me" (verse 6). Some will object to such an exclusive statement. However, who else came back from the grave? Who else lived a sinless life? Who else so transformed ethics, leadership, politics, and social justice? There's no other who has shown us who God is and offered us a path to his presence (John 1:18; Acts 4:12; Hebrews 1:3).

2. The Promise of Success Through the Spirit

The disciples couldn't imagine carrying out Jesus's mission without him. However, Jesus saw more clearly: "Truly, truly, I say to you, whoever believes in me will also do the works that I do; and greater works than these will he do" (John 14:12). How in the world is that possible? Can we do greater works than Jesus himself? Yes, he said we would. And Jesus's followers have vastly expanded his ministry: the number of converts, breadth of geography, depth of social justice, height of political influence, and weight of cultural impact. How did all this happen? Jesus identified two resources driving our impact:

1. **Prayer.** Because we're God's children and not just servants, our prayers have massive impact. As Jesus said, we could ask anything in his name and get a yes from God (verses 13–14). This promise is repeated in John 15:7, 16; 16:23–26; 1 John 3:22; 5:14–15. Obviously, this blank check is not for personal gain but for mission-critical tasks. If we ask the Father for what we need to build Jesus's kingdom, we're going to get a yes. It may not come in our time frame, but it will come every time.

2. **The Spirit.** More importantly, Jesus would ask the Father to send us the Helper (John 14:16). This Greek word, *paraklētos,* means "called alongside." The Holy Spirit comes alongside us. He's our coach, mentor, and guide. He comforts, leads, helps, protects, encourages, and convicts. Jesus promised, "He dwells with you and will be in you" (verse 17). On earth, Jesus was limited to one place at a time. After his ascension, the Father sent the omnipresent Spirit to be with each of us all the time. Through the Spirit, we have personal access to Jesus and to our Father. The Spirit and prayer go hand in hand to ensure we complete Jesus' commission.

3. The Promise of Love in Jesus

"Whoever has my commandments and keeps them, he it is who *loves* me. And he who *loves* me will be *loved* by my Father, and I will *love* him and manifest myself to him" (verse 21).

Judas (not Iscariot) was confused: "Lord, how is it that you will manifest yourself to us, and not to the world?" (verse 22). At first glance, Jesus's answer seems irrelevant: "If anyone loves me, he will keep my word" (verse 23). How did that answer the question about why Jesus would reveal himself to insiders and not outsiders? Here's how: it's in obeying Jesus that we fully see Jesus. Only when we do what he says do we fully experience his presence and power. That's why Jesus added, "The Helper, the Holy Spirit, whom the Father will send in my name, he will teach you all things and bring to your remembrance all that I have said to you" (verse 26).

This brings us full circle: "Peace I leave with you; my peace I give to you. Not as the world gives do I give to you. Let not your hearts be troubled, neither let them be afraid" (verse 27). Our peace during trouble comes from Jesus's presence. God became present in the person of Jesus. And when Jesus left, his presence remained with us through his Spirit living in us.

Key Points

- Jesus promised to prepare a place for us. That means he's making a way for us to have an eternal relationship with the Father.

- The Holy Spirit is our advocate, coming alongside us so we can carry out Jesus's mission.

- When we obey Jesus's commands, the Holy Spirit empowers us to experience the love of the Father.

This Week

❏ **Day 1 (Eyes):** After reading the essay, answer this question: What hope do you need?

❏ **Day 2 (Ears):** What was promised through the coming of the Holy Spirit in Joel 2:28–32 and Ezekiel 36:22–36?

❏ **Day 3 (Heart):** Think about John 1:18, Acts 4:12, and Hebrews 1:3. How is Jesus exclusively the way to the Father?

❏ **Day 4 (Voice):** Discussion:

- Share about a time when you felt alone or abandoned.
- What is it that makes Jesus uniquely qualified to introduce people to God?
- Have you ever experienced the power or presence of the Spirit? What was that like?
- How do you sense the Spirit guiding you? Mentors, Scripture, music, friends, parents?

❏ **Day 5 (Hands):** Ask God for something you need to fulfill his mission.

45

How Can We Learn Grit from How Jesus Suffered?

Biblical Concept: Suffering
Read: Mark 14:32–52

It all started in a garden. The Garden of Eden. There it all went wrong when Satan temped Adam and Eve. Their bite of betrayal brought death and destruction into the world. Here we are again in a garden. Jesus prayed in the face of death and destruction. His obedience would reverse the curse of a world that betrayed God. His suffering started here.

Gethsemane

The Garden of Gethsemane is an olive grove on the Mount of Olives. It faces Jerusalem and is one of the only quiet places near the city. Jesus took Peter, James, and John into the garden. He wanted his support group with him. He told them, "My soul is very sorrowful, even to death. Remain here and watch" (Mark 14:34). This may be more literal than we think. Luke, the physician, noted that "his sweat became like great drops of blood falling down to the ground" (Luke 22:44). This may indicate a medical condition called hematidrosis where capillaries burst and a person sweats blood. Jesus was in real trouble.

In agony, he fell on his knees (Luke 22:41), then on his face (Matthew 26:39), and prayed, "Abba, Father, all things are possible for you. *Remove this cup from me*" (Mark 14:36). The cup in the Old Testament is a symbol of God's wrath (Jeremiah 25:15–16). Jesus was about to absorb *the wrath of God* and feel separation from his Father. He would become sin itself (2 Corinthians 5:21), and it was killing him. Yet he was committed to obeying God's will even as his heart was breaking and his body was breaking down.

Jesus needed the support of his friends. He went to them but found them asleep. What Jesus told Peter he could say to most of us: "The spirit indeed is willing, but the flesh is weak" (Matthew 26:41). In Jesus's view, prayer is more important than sleep, especially when we're facing significant trials. Perhaps the reason we can't keep our promises to Jesus is that we don't stay awake with him in prayer.

Allow me one quick observation. Often we think there's something wrong with us when God says no to our requests. Yet he said no to Jesus in the garden—three times. If God says no to you, you're in pretty good company. You may, in fact, be exactly where God wants you.

Three times Jesus prayed, "Remove this cup from me. Yet not what I will, but what you will" (Mark 14:36). In that sliver of time between Jesus's request and his submission, our eternal salvation hung in the balance. No one could force Jesus to the cross. It was his submission to the Father that won our salvation. Likewise, if we don't submit to God's will, the world may never know the love of Christ, who died for their sins.

The Kiss of Death

After finding his friends asleep for the third time, Jesus said, "Rise, let us be going; see, my betrayer is at hand" (verse 42). Then "Judas came, one of the twelve, and with him a crowd with swords and clubs, from the chief priests and the scribes and the elders" (verse 43).

Judas likely led the soldiers first to Mary's house, where the Last Supper was held. Jesus had gone. So Iscariot led them to the garden where he knew Jesus frequently prayed. John Mark, the author of the gospel, was likely a teen at the time. He might have heard the pounding on the door of his home and the conversation of the men looking for Jesus. He was a smart kid; he figured out where Jesus had gone and set out on a dead run to warn him. But by the time he got to the garden, it was too late. More on this in a moment.

When the disciples saw Judas through the flickering light of the soldiers' torches, it suddenly sank in exactly what he was doing. Jesus broke the silence: "Whom do you seek?" (John 18:4). "Jesus of Nazareth," they replied. "I am he," Jesus confessed, making Judas's kiss unnecessary (verse 5). He still stepped forward. "Rabbi!" Judas said as he kissed him (Mark 14:45)—a normal greeting for men in the Middle East.

Jesus was immediately arrested. Peter would have none of it. Wielding a sword, he took a quick swipe at Malchus, the servant of the high priest (John 18:10). Malchus dodged the blow, but the sword still glanced off his skull, severing his ear. Jesus ordered Peter to put away his sword: "All who take the sword will perish by the sword" (Matthew 26:52). Only Luke, the physician, described how Jesus miraculously healed Malchus, snapping his ear back on like a Lego block (22:51)! If you were the soldiers arresting Jesus, you would have just gotten really nervous. And Peter just got away with assault because there was no longer any evidence of his crime.

Jesus turned his rebuke to the chief priests: "Have you come out as against a robber, with swords and clubs to capture me? Day after day I was with you in the temple teaching, and you did not seize me" (Mark 14:48–49). He accused them of false arrest and cowardice for coming at him at night rather than in the light of day in the temple they supposedly controlled. With that, the apostles fled, leaving Jesus alone in the dark.

Some young man was there wearing only his linen tunic. The soldiers grabbed ahold of his garment. He slipped out of it, then ran naked into the night. Who was this streaker? Who else would care about this strange eyewitness detail except John Mark, the author of the book? The point of this curious detail is that Jesus was desperately alone, abandoned by his closest friends. One even endured the shame of nakedness to get away.

Suffering isn't the hard part. Suffering alone is. Because Jesus suffered alone in the Garden of Gethsemane, our curse from the Garden of Eden was reversed so that we will never suffer separation from our God. Jesus modeled courageous suffering. Are you following his example?

Key Points

- Jesus's suffering began in Gethsemane.
- Three times he prayed to be released from the Cross. God said no.
- Even Jesus's best friends fled, leaving him alone in the dark with his enemies.

This Week

❏ **Day 1 (Eyes):** As you read the essay, what did you learn about how to go through suffering?

❏ **Day 2 (Ears):** What are the similarities between Gethsemane and Absalom betraying David in 2 Samuel 15?

❏ **Day 3 (Heart):** Think about Romans 8:17, Colossians 1:24, and 1 Peter 2:21–23. How can suffering make you tougher?

❏ **Day 4 (Voice):** Discussion:
- What's the most difficult thing you've ever had to endure?
- How did you pray differently during that difficult time?
- Based on Jesus's suffering, what advice would you give to others who are suffering?
- What would make you better able to endure times of trouble?

❏ **Day 5 (Hands):** Offer to be present with someone who is suffering so that she isn't alone.

46

How Do You Stay in Control in a Crisis?

Biblical Concept: Opposition
Read: Mark 14:53–72

Criminal Minds, Law & Order, and *The Blacklist.* There, I confessed it; I'm obsessed with crime shows. When bad guys get what they deserve, something in me rejoices. However, it's not always clear who the bad guys are. Even the good guys have moral flaws, and the bad guys have some redeeming qualities. So it is in this biblical story of Caiaphas and Peter. Jesus alone seems to have had integrity amid crisis, and that gave him control when everyone else was spinning out of control. There's a lesson here that most of us desperately need to learn.

The Trial of Jesus

After his arrest, Jesus was taken to the high priest, Caiaphas, the highest official in Israel. Caiaphas was on top of the political pyramid and the primary ambassador between the people and the Roman governor, who reported to the emperor.

As an interesting aside, a first-century ossuary (a box used to collect the bones of someone who died) was found in Jerusalem with *Caiaphas* inscribed on the lid. Most scholars agree that this box contains the bones of the biblical high priest who condemned Jesus to death. Incredible! We have the burial box of the man who put Jesus to death, while Jesus's grave is empty.

Back to the story. First Caiaphas arranged a string of "witnesses" to accuse Jesus. But they couldn't get their stories straight. They were contradicting one another. Caiaphas was at risk of having to acquit Jesus.

So Caiaphas intervened: "Are you the Christ, the Son of the Blessed?" (Mark 14:61). Well, that was a problem. Jewish judges weren't allowed to ask defendants to incriminate themselves. There were ten distinct violations of Jewish legal rules in this trial:

- Jesus was arrested through a bribe.

- He was arrested without a specific charge.

- The trial was held at night.

- There were false witnesses with conflicting stories.

- He wasn't allowed to cross-examine the witnesses.

- He was asked to incriminate himself.

- The high priest declared his sentence without first asking for a vote.

- He was struck in the face during the trial without just cause.

- The charges against him were changed when he was transferred to Pilate.

- He was convicted and sentenced on the same day.

Even though Caiaphas was out of line asking Jesus to incriminate himself, Jesus answered his question. The high priest asked, "Are you the Christ, the Son of the Blessed?" Jesus said, "I am" (verse 62), which, in Hebrew, is the name of God: Yahweh. Oh boy. Then he added, "You will see the Son of Man seated at the right hand of Power, and coming with the clouds of heaven" (verse 62). This triggered a violent response.

Caiaphas tore his robe, which was a powerful expression of grief (Genesis 37:29; 2 Kings 18:37). "That's blasphemy!" he roared. So the punishment began. The soldiers played a game something like blindman's buff. They beat Jesus with their fists and with a rod and even spit on him. Then they asked him to reveal who did it. According to Isaiah 52:14, he was beaten beyond recognition. Jesus's trial was going badly; Peter's was going worse.

The Trial of Peter

While Jesus was on trial inside the palace, Peter was on trial in the courtyard.

There he was, warming himself by the fire. The girl watching the gate recognized him as a follower of Jesus. The little blabbermouth came right up to him and said, "You also were with the Nazarene, Jesus" (Mark 14:67). "I have no idea what you mean," Peter said. Big fat lie. Peter was on a secret mission, likely to somehow create an escape for Jesus. Why else would he have been there?

He walked away from the fire and into the shadows by the gate. They were less likely to identify him there. But that pesky girl started pointing at him, telling the soldiers, "This man is one of them" (verse 69). Peter was louder this time: "I swear to God I don't know the man." That bought him a bit of time, but in the crowd was a relative of Malchus (John 18:26). He identified Peter beyond a shadow of a doubt. Peter called down curses upon himself (Matthew 26:74), swearing a third time he didn't know Jesus (Matthew 26:74).

In that moment, two things happened. The rooster crowed (a second time, according to Mark), reminding Peter of Jesus's words. That shrill cry woke Peter, and he realized he had just denied Jesus, the very thing he had sworn he would never do. His motives were likely good—trying to help Jesus escape. But because he took matters into his own hands rather than trusting God's plan, he was forced into a situation in which there were no good options.

The second thing that happened was even more difficult for Peter. When the rooster crowed, Jesus turned and caught Peter's eye (Luke 22:61). He knew that Jesus knew exactly what he had done. Peter broke down and wept. Mark's wording expresses utter brokenness (14:72). He was undone by what he had done. In Jesus's worst moment, Peter had let him down in the worst way.

There's a lesson here for us: Jesus was in total control even when he was being railroaded. Peter lost control by trying to take control. What was the difference between them? Because Peter was asleep in the garden, he was confused in the courtyard. Jesus, on the other hand, prepared for the crisis in prayer. It was on his knees that he battled for control. He prayed, "Not my will, but yours" (Luke 22:42). Once he submitted to God's will, he was in control of every situation he faced. Submission to God in prayer is the preparation we need for any crisis.

Key Points

- The trial of Jesus was unjust and illegal, yet Jesus submitted to it.

- Peter lost control in the courtyard because he tried to take control.

- Jesus was in control of the trial because he determined in the garden to submit to God's will.

This Week

❑ **Day I (Eyes):** After reading the essay, answer this question: How do you respond in crisis?

❑ **Day 2 (Ears):** There was a pit in Caiaphas's house where Jesus was likely held. When people visit the site today, they're encouraged to read Psalm 88. Read it now, thinking about Jesus in that dungeon.

❑ **Day 3 (Heart):** Think about what these verses say about crisis: 2 Corinthians 4:16–18, Hebrews 2:18, and James 1:2–4.

❑ **Day 4 (Voice):** Discussion:
- Share about a time when you were mistreated. How did you handle it?
- What advice would you give to a friend who was mistreated at school? Do you follow that advice?
- What are you trying to control right now that you need to give over to God?
- Are there actions you need to take in this crisis that you're procrastinating on?

❑ **Day 5 (Hands):** Spend thirty minutes praying over a crisis in your life. Ask God for strength to control what you can, and release the rest to God's control.

47

How Do You Endure Pain?

Biblical Concept: Endurance
Read: Matthew 27:11–26

The trial of Jesus was filled with false accusations, rejection, and pain. If you know what that feels like, you're not alone. Jesus's example paved the way for our endurance. For a moment, let's look at what was happening behind the scenes of his trial.

Caiaphas, the high priest, sentenced Jesus to death for blasphemy (cursing God), but he had no authority to execute capital punishment. That would have to come from Pilate, the Roman governor at the time.

The locals had a bitter history with Pilate. Early in his administration, he tried to install shields honoring the emperor in Herod's palace in Jerusalem. Jewish nationalists threw a fit and forced him to take them down by appealing to the emperor. Then we learn from Luke 13:1 that Pilate killed some Galileans while they were making a sacrifice in the temple—not cool. Their political climate was tense to say the least.

Plus, Pilate's personal history back in Rome was sketchy. He was "skating on thin ice," as my mom always said. Pilate was vulnerable if the Jewish leaders reported any misconduct. So they used that to their advantage while accusing Jesus.

Endure False Accusations with Faith

The Jewish leaders told Pilate, "We found this man misleading our nation and forbidding us to give tribute to Caesar, and saying that he himself is Christ, a king" (Luke 23:2). Charge 1: he misled the nation—rebellion. Rome didn't hesitate to punish those who disturbed the peace. However, the Jewish leaders were causing as much of a disturbance as Jesus. Charge 2: he forbade Jews to pay taxes. False! Jesus told a crowd in the temple to give to Caesar what was Caesar's (Matthew 22:15–22). Charge 3: he claimed to be king. Absolutely true and 100 percent lethal if he was convicted. So that was the charge Pilate investigated.

Pilate asked, "Are you the King of the Jews?" Jesus's reply is puzzling: "You have said so" (Matthew 27:11). It's like he was saying, "You're the one saying that, not me." John shared a helpful detail: Jesus asked, "Do you say this of your own accord, or did others say it to you about me?" (18:34). He was trying to figure out what Pilate meant by *king*. Was he a king challenging the emperor? No. Was he King of the Jews, the promised Messiah? Yes. Pilate acted as if Jesus were being argumentative: "Do you not hear how many things they testify against you?" (Matthew 27:13). He wasn't being argumentative; he was simply trying to be clear. Answering irrelevant accusations wouldn't solve the problem. Jesus did what few of us can manage in the face of opposition. He was silent (Isaiah 53:7). He didn't answer a single false accusation. Pilate was "greatly amazed" and should have been (Matthew 27:14). We would do well to follow Jesus's example. The more we defend ourselves, the more ammunition we offer to our enemies.

How can we endure false accusations? With faith in God's goodness. Throughout the Bible, the righteous were always vindicated, whether in this life or the next. Eventually the evil of those who pretend to be righteous will be exposed and people will see your innocence. Our faith in God allows us to stand firm in the face of false accusations.

Endure Rejection with Hope

Pilate's wife interrupted the proceedings with an urgent message: "Have nothing to do with that righteous man, for I have suffered much because of him today in a dream" (verse 19). In the ancient world, dreams were interpreted not as subconscious concerns but as messages from the gods. Pilate now had divine confirmation of his own intuition—Jesus was innocent. He knew the Jewish leaders had delivered Jesus up out of envy (verse 18).

Pilate attempted to release Jesus using something like a presidential pardon. By releasing a prisoner, he gained approval from the crowd. He pitted Jesus against a rebel named Barabbas. Jesus preached peace; Barabbas promoted violence. Pilate surely had heard of Jesus's popularity with the people, yet today the leaders controlled the crowd in the courtyard (verse 20). The crowd's cry was clear: "Barabbas" (verse 21). Jesus would take his place on a cross between two rebels who were likely companions of Barabbas.

Jesus had now been rejected by Judas, Peter, Pilate, and the crowds who had declared him king just five days earlier. How do you endure that kind of rejection? You hope. Hope is the flip side of faith. While faith looks back on the faithfulness of God, hope looks forward, past your present pain, to trust that God will defend you and can even save your enemy.

Endure Pain with Love

Pilate then asked, "What shall I do with Jesus who is called Christ?" (verse 22). The crowd cried in unison, sounding like a chorus from hell: "Crucify him!" In frustration Pilate thundered back, "Why? What evil has he done?" (verse 23). They simply shouted louder, "Crucify him!" Then the Jewish leaders told Pilate, "If you release this man, you are not Caesar's friend. Everyone who makes himself a king opposes Caesar" (John 19:12). That was blackmail. They played to Pilate's weak relationship with the emperor. Dirty but effective.

Pilate washed his hands, rejecting any blame for the execution. "I am innocent of this man's blood; see to it yourselves," he said (Matthew 27:24). The people responded, "His blood be on us and on our children!" (verse 25). Be careful what you ask for; you might just get it.

We must remember, Jesus didn't die because of his enemies' wicked plot. He chose this in the garden. He suffered *for* us, not just *because* of us. He loved Peter and Pilate, Judas and the Jews who killed him. His suffering brought salvation. Ours can too. We endure because we know that our suffering can bring hope, healing, and forgiveness. Grit and determination can take you only so far through pain. Love knows no bounds.

Key Points

- Righteousness is always vindicated. We can endure false accusations if we have faith in God's goodness.

- There's no pain worse than rejection. Hope pushes faith forward, past the pain. We trust that God will defend us and can even save our enemies.

- Loving our enemies has greater power than grit to enable us to endure pain.

This Week

❏ **Day 1 (Eyes):** After reading the essay, answer this question: How is your level of faith, hope, and love?

❏ **Day 2 (Ears):** What predictions from Isaiah 52:13–53:12 were fulfilled in Jesus's execution?

❏ **Day 3 (Heart):** Think about how God treats his enemies and how we should imitate him: Romans 5:10, Romans 12:20, and Hebrews 10:12–13.

❏ **Day 4 (Voice):** Discussion:

- Have you ever been rejected, betrayed, or hated? What was that like?
- What can you do to show love in action to a person who has rejected you?
- Are there any specific strategies that Jesus used at his trial that you could offer as advice to a friend who has been rejected, betrayed, or mistreated?
- How can the pain we endure increase the faith, hope, and love of others?

❏ **Day 5 (Hands):** Write out a prayer that you would want your enemies to pray for you (three sentences). Now pray it for your enemies.

48

Why Did Jesus Die?

Biblical Concept: Atonement
Read: Matthew 27:27–54

The Bible begins with a garden. There sin damaged God's good creation. The Bible ends with a new world, where God will restore creation. The Cross bridges that great divide. Jesus's death paid the penalty for our sins. It restores our souls and promises a new world, where all will be set right.

Before the Cross

Before Jesus was ever on the cross, the soldiers beat him beyond human recognition (Isaiah 52:14). They used a flagellum, a stick about eighteen inches long with leather strands, each embedded with sharp objects such as glass, metal, or sheep's knucklebones. The victim was stripped naked and tied to a pillar. A soldier on either side slapped the strands against the flesh, then pulled down sharply, scraping or ripping the victim's back, buttocks, and legs. The strands also wrapped around the victim, lacerating the quads, abs, and chest and often gouging out the eyes. Six out of ten men died from flogging alone, sometimes because of loss of blood. At other times their insides literally fell out of the gaping wounds in their torsos.

Jesus's flogging was followed by a mock coronation. The soldiers dressed him in a scarlet robe. After twisting together thorns, they pressed this "crown" into his skull. Using fists trained for battle, they punched his face while mocking him: "Hail, King of the Jews!" (Matthew 27:29).

Afterward, they ripped the robe from his back, reopening the wounds. They replaced it with a *patibulum*—the hundred-pound crossbar of the cross. They made Jesus carry it through narrow streets to a place called Golgotha, meaning "place of a skull."

Ahead of the procession walked a Roman soldier carrying the *titulus,* a sign that clearly spelled out the charges against the victim. The charges read, "Jesus of Nazareth, the King of the Jews," translated into Aramaic, Greek, and Latin (John 19:19–20). No one could miss it.

On the Cross

Oddly, there are no details of the Crucifixion itself. This wasn't the kind of thing people talked about in polite company. Besides, once you had seen one, no one needed to describe it. Regardless, Jesus's physical pain isn't the point. His spiritual suffering was far greater than physical torture. Jesus took our place; he became our sin, and he was separated from God.

The Romans perfected the "art" of crucifixion to prolong the agony of the execution. By driving nails through the wristbones, no essential arteries were severed, but the median nerves were, sending searing agony through the shoulder blades. Four- to five-inch spikes, likewise, were nailed through the calcanei (heel bones), sending similar pain through the pelvis.

People who were crucified typically lasted several days. Birds of prey would peck at the helpless victims' eyes while wild dogs tore at their open wounds. Crucifixion victims died from stress to their bodies. In Jesus's case his heart burst. How do we know? When the soldier pierced his side, blood and water flowed out. This indicates that his heart ruptured and the blood from the ventricles pumped into the fluid of the sac around his heart. Jesus literally died of a broken heart.

Around the Cross

Jesus's executioners intended to shame him by crucifying a criminal on either side of him. But by doing so, they fulfilled Isaiah 53:9, showing God's hand in his death. Likewise, when the guards gambled for his garments, they followed God's script of the execution (Psalm 22:18).

Those who passed by shook their heads and said, "You who would destroy the temple and rebuild it in three days, save yourself! If you are the Son of God, come down from the cross" (Matthew 27:40). The leaders joined in ridiculing him: "He saved others; he cannot save himself" (verse 42). That was true, but not how they intended. Jesus couldn't save others *and* save himself. His sufferings gave us our salvation.

The soldiers joined the crowds in mocking Jesus (Luke 23:36). Even those on the crosses next to him taunted him. They suggested Jesus should save himself *and* them (Matthew 27:44; Luke 23:39)! The whole mob thought they were being clever, but they were quoting *and fulfilling* Scripture (Psalm 22:7–8).

From the Cross

In the midst of agony, Jesus spoke seven times from the cross. Sayings 1, 4, and 7 were addressed to his Father. Sayings 2, 3, 5, and 6 were for the benefit of his disciples. Let's eavesdrop on his "deathbed" conversations:

> **Saying 1: "Father, forgive them, for they know not what they do"** (Luke 23:34). This was not exactly a king's pardon (Acts 3:17; 1 Corinthians 2:8) but an offer of redemption to all who would accept him by faith (John 3:16–17; Romans 6:23; 1 Peter 2:24).

Saying 2: "Today you will be with me in paradise" (Luke 23:43). One of the bandits ridiculed Jesus with the rest of the crowd. His partner, pinned on the other side of Jesus, rebuked him: "Do you not fear God, since you are under the same sentence of condemnation?" (verse 40). Then he said to Jesus, "Remember me when you come into your kingdom" (verse 42). Jesus promised him salvation.

Saying 3: "Woman, behold, your son! . . . Behold, your mother!" (John 19:26–27). Among the crazed crowd were a few faithful followers. Jesus's mother was one of them. He gave Mary into the care of John, his closest believing relative. History suggests John cared for her until her death.

Saying 4: "My God, my God, why have you forsaken me?" (Matthew 27:46; Mark 15:34). Jesus was quoting Psalm 22:1. Psalm 22 is the most detailed description of crucifixion in all ancient literature, *and* it was composed six hundred years before crucifixion was practiced! Many ask why God turned his back on Jesus. As 2 Corinthians 5:21 explains, "He made him to be sin who knew no sin, so that in him we might become the righteousness of God." This rejection wasn't permanent (Acts 2:27, 31), but it was necessary to overcome sin and death.

Saying 5: "I thirst" (John 19:28). This may seem like an unnecessary detail. However, John clarified that it fulfilled a prophecy from Psalm 69:21: "For my thirst they gave me sour wine to drink." The soldiers dipped a sponge into their vinegar wine and lifted it on a flimsy hyssop branch (Jesus was likely not more than two feet off the ground).

Saying 6: "It is finished" (John 19:30). The Greek word translated "finished" is interesting. It can describe a task accomplished, a dangerous feat performed, a promise fulfilled, an order executed, or an oath kept, but the most interesting meaning, I think, is a debt paid. "When Christ had offered for all time a single sacrifice for sins, he sat down at the right hand of God" (Hebrews 10:12).

Saying 7: "Father, into your hands I commit my spirit!" (Luke 23:46). This is a quote from Psalm 31:5, but the entire psalm is a commentary on his experience (verses 2, 4–5, 7, 11–14, 22, 24). With his final breath, he cried out to his Father, affirming his faith. He had finished his mission. He lived a perfect life and died as an atoning sacrifice.

Every detail, every word fulfilled the ancient prophecies and God's eternal plan. The Lamb of God paid the price for the sins of the world. Jesus's death redeemed us. At long last, the curse of Eden could be lifted.

Key Points

- The cross of Christ is the centerpiece of the entire Bible.
- Each detail of the Crucifixion fulfilled a prophecy.
- Jesus paid the price for our sins.

This Week

❏ **Day 1 (Eyes):** After reading the essay, how would you describe what Jesus did for you?

❏ **Day 2 (Ears):** Read Psalm 22. Underline every phrase that describes the crucifixion of Jesus.

❏ **Day 3 (Heart):** Think about what Jesus accomplished for us on the cross: Romans 3:21–26, 2 Corinthians 5:21, and Hebrews 9:26–28.

❏ **Day 4 (Voice):** Discussion:

- What is the greatest sacrifice that anyone has made for you (other than Jesus)? What motivated that person to make that sacrifice?
- Of those surrounding the cross, whom do you relate to most? Can you feel what that person might have felt?
- The cross of Jesus should make us feel grateful, loyal, and free. Which of these three do you demonstrate the most?
- If his cross covers *all* our sins, what should we do, feel, and say about the cross?

❏ **Day 5 (Hands):** If you have any sins that you're still holding on to, have a private ceremony in which you write them on a piece of paper, then burn it (safely) to fully and finally release them to Jesus.

49

Did Jesus Really Rise from the Dead?

Biblical Concept: Resurrection
Read: John 20

Just as the Cross is the center of the Bible, the Resurrection is the foundation of our faith. In short, "if Christ has not been raised, then our preaching is in vain and your faith is in vain" (1 Corinthians 15:14). The death and resurrection of Jesus are two sides of the same coin. They are Christianity in a nutshell.

Through the Eyes of Insiders

It was Sunday morning. At sunrise, Mary Magdalene and the other women gathered their ointment and headed to the edge of town to anoint Jesus's dead body. When they arrived, the stone was already rolled away. The body was gone! Mary instinctively raced to inform the apostles. Still breathless, she blurted out, "They have taken the Lord out of the tomb, and we do not know where they have laid him" (John 20:2).

Peter and John rushed to the tomb to survey the situation. John, racing ahead of Peter, got there first and peered into the tomb; the body was, in fact, missing. Who would defile Jesus's corpse by moving it? No one had motive or opportunity! Even worse, the linen wrappings were still on the stone where the body had been laid, and the head covering neatly folded. Who would take the time to strip Jesus's body naked before stealing it?

When Peter arrived, he pushed past John at the entrance. John entered after him and began to believe. He began to put the prophetic pieces together. After all, Scripture promises the Resurrection (Psalm 16:10; Isaiah 53:10–11; Hosea 6:1–2).

Through the Eyes of an Outsider

Peter and John returned to their hideout, wondering what all this could mean. Mary, who had come back to the tomb, remained there wailing. Two angels, dressed in white, sat at the head and feet of where Jesus had been laid. From their perspective, weeping was the last thing she should have been doing. They didn't understand her emotion, and she didn't comprehend their identity. "Why are you weeping?" they asked. It seemed obvious to Mary: "They have taken away my Lord, and I do not know where they have laid him" (John 20:13). Before the angels answered, she turned away, only to encounter a "gardener." Jesus repeated the question: "Woman, why are you weeping? Whom are you seeking?" She replied, "Sir, if you have carried him away, tell me where you have laid him, and I will take him away" (verse 15).

Jesus's one-word reply opened her eyes: "Mary." There must have been something in the way he said her name. So many men had called her name, but none with the love and dignity Jesus gave her. She recognized him immediately and cried out in her native Aramaic, "Rabboni!" ("teacher"). Mary latched on (verse 16). Jesus responded, "Do not cling to me, for I have not yet ascended to the Father; but go to my brothers and say to them, 'I am ascending to my Father and your Father, to my God and your God'" (verse 17).

There was no time to hang on to the moment. She had work to do—important work. She was the very first witness to the Resurrection. Think about that. This was the single greatest announcement in human history, and all four Gospels agree that the honor was given to Mary. At that time, women were property, not witnesses. And this particular woman had a sketchy past. Let this truth sink into your soul: Jesus has a role for you, an honorable role, regardless of your past or position. Mary ran to the upper room and announced, "I have seen the Lord" (verse 18). They thought she had lost her mind (Luke 24:11).

No one expected Jesus to rise from the dead, even though he had predicted it several times (Matthew 16:21; 17:23; 20:19). The Greeks and Romans didn't believe in resurrection, nor did they want one. They wanted to shed their bodies with all their frailty and suffering. Some Jews believed in resurrection, but only at the end of time. No one believed that an individual in this space and time would rise from the dead. No one.

Through the Eyes of a Skeptic

The apostles were fugitives. They were hiding in the upper room with the door locked. It was Sunday evening, and their hearts stopped when someone started beating on the door. They were terrified that soldiers had come to arrest them, but then they heard the familiar voices of friends. Two disciples had run seven miles from their home in Emmaus. They sounded as crazy as the women. "The Lord has risen indeed," they cried breathlessly. Ten apostles, minus Judas Iscariot and Thomas, discussed wildly what this could mean.

They were cut short by another familiar voice: "Peace be with you" (John 20:19). They turned in awe at what they saw. They thought they were seeing a ghost (Luke 24:37). After all, Jesus had just passed through a locked door (John 20:19). He extended his hands to show the scars and lifted his tunic to show where the spear had punctured his side. They were stunned. Jesus asked whether they had anything to eat. Someone handed him a piece of fish. He ate it as evidence; apparently ghosts don't do that.

They were still speechless, so Jesus began again: "Peace be with you.

As the Father has sent me, even so I am sending you" (verse 21). It was no longer a greeting; it was a commission—and not just a commission but empowerment as well. He breathed on them, saying, "Receive the Holy Spirit" (verse 22). This was what Jesus had promised (John 7:39; 16:7). The Holy Spirit would empower them to preach the gospel. Jesus's resurrection results in our mission—always!

Thomas missed the whole thing. You can imagine the excitement when he returned: "We have seen the Lord" (John 20:25). Doubtful, he protested, "Unless I see in his hands the mark of the nails, and place my finger into the mark of the nails, and place my hand into his side, I will never believe" (verse 25). Make no mistake: Thomas was loyal and brave; he had proved that (John 11:16; 14:5). He just couldn't believe without seeing for himself. To be fair, no one else did either, except possibly John. So let's not be too tough on Thomas. After all, we are him.

The next eight days had to be terrible for Thomas. Everyone else was giddy; he was grumpy. Then it happened. Just as before, Jesus appeared behind a locked door. Same greeting: "Peace be with you" (20:26). Jesus even used Thomas's words from a week before: "Put your finger here, and see my hands; and put out your hand, and place it in my side. Do not disbelieve, but believe" (verse 27). Thomas believed. Boy, did he believe! His confession topped every previous one. In fact, in the history of Israel, no Jew had ever said this to another human being: "My Lord and my God!" (verse 28).

Jesus spoke to Thomas but also to us. Listen in: "Have you believed because you have seen me? Blessed are those who have not seen and yet have believed" (verse 29). Don't miss this. All the evidence we need to believe is *already given* in John's gospel: "Jesus did many other signs in the presence of the disciples, which are not written in this book; but these are written so that you may believe that Jesus is the Christ, the Son of God, and that by believing you may have life in his name" (verses 30–31). The purpose of John's gospel is to give us all the reason we need to believe. And if we believe, we will have life in Jesus's name.

You Decide

Volumes have been written on the evidence for the Resurrection. Let me offer here the barest summary. To those who say no one can rise from the dead, let me humbly suggest that you already believe that it's possible. You believe that life sprang forth from nonlife, whether it was an evolutionary process or the action of a Creator. So the real question is whether the evidence suggests that it happened again with Jesus. Any fair historical quest must reasonably answer four questions:

1. Why did the early Christians never honor the tomb of Jesus? After all, Jews were known for honoring the graves of loved ones.
2. How do we account for the radical change in Peter (coward to courageous), Thomas (doubter to shouter), Paul (persecutor to preacher), James (opposing to leading), and John (hothead to humble)? And why did ten of the eleven apostles die as martyrs for their proclamation of the Resurrection if it never happened?
3. Why did the Resurrection become the centerpiece of Christian faith when people of that era didn't believe it could happen in their own lifetime?
4. What accounts for a Jewish church moving worship from Sabbath to Sunday and adding baptism and the Lord's Supper, both of which proclaim the Resurrection?

There's plenty of evidence if you want to believe and an eternal reward if you do.

Key Points

- Jesus's followers never honored his tomb because it was empty.

- The accounts of the Resurrection are neither fiction nor fabricated.

- Every key leader of the church was radically transformed by the Resurrection.

- The church itself requires a resurrection for Sunday worship, communion, baptism, and the core of its original preaching.

This Week

❏ **Day 1 (Eyes):** After reading the essay, answer this question: Have you considered the Resurrection the core of your faith?

❏ **Day 2 (Ears):** Read Psalm 16. Research where verses 8–11 are quoted in the New Testament.

❏ **Day 3 (Heart):** Think about what 1 Corinthians 15:3–8, 1 Thessalonians 4:14, and 1 John 1:1–2 teach about the Resurrection.

❏ **Day 4 (Voice):** Discussion:

- Share something that you believe only because you saw it.
- What person in this story do you relate to most? Why?
- What evidence for the Resurrection is most compelling to you?
- Share a doubt that you have or have had about your faith. Now share why you might doubt that doubt.

❏ **Day 5 (Hands):** Make a short list of why you believe in the resurrection of Jesus. Share it with a pastor who can help sharpen it; then share it with a friend.

50

What Does Jesus Expect Us to Do Now?

Biblical Concept: Commission
Read: Matthew 28:16–20

To be honest, even after decades of ministry, talking about Jesus—especially with my family—can be scary. But Jesus is worth the risk. If he could lay his life down for us, we can lay our reputations on the line for him. This was Jesus's final command before leaving this earth, and it was based on one simple fact: "All authority in heaven and on earth has been given to me" (Matthew 28:18). He is the universal Lord. And that takes a lot of pressure off us. Our job is not to "win the world" but simply to make Jesus famous in our circles. So, what *exactly* does Jesus expect from us?

Make Disciples

Jesus said, "Make disciples" (verse 19). Simply put, a disciple is a learner—an apprentice who imitates what you do. So discipleship begins by inviting someone into your life. He needs to be with you during school, after school, and while you're walking the mall or watching sports. Many think discipleship is face-to-face Bible study. That's part of it, but discipleship is more shoulder-to-shoulder modeling of Jesus's life.

It's more than teaching what Jesus said. It's *living* how Jesus *lived:* loving God and loving people. It's that simple, but it isn't that easy. Loving God covers a range of disciplines, beginning with baptism and including prayer, Bible reading, confession, fasting, meditation, and service. Loving others includes forgiveness, hanging out, generosity, and confrontation, among other disciplines.

Obviously, we can't do everything at once. It's a process. The word *disciple* is used 269 times in 253 verses in the New Testament. Based on those verses, here's a summary of what it takes to be a disciple. Pay attention to what body parts are required to do what Jesus asked:

1. **Investigation: eyes and feet.** In John 1:39, Jesus gave an invitation: "Come and you will see." The initial stage of discipleship really is that simple. Hang out long enough to see whether this is something you want to commit to. Fifty-nine times, discipleship is described as following Jesus—being where he was. Another ten times, it required seeing what he was doing.

2. **Instruction: ears and mouth.** Second, we are to listen to what Jesus says and ask questions for clarification. Forty-three times, the Gospels describe the disciples listening to Jesus. Thirty-seven times, they asked questions or made a statement (which Jesus usually had to correct). Keep in mind that it isn't enough to know Bible trivia. Our goal is to know Jesus personally.

3. **Application: hands.** Simply put, a disciple does what Jesus does. Fifty-eight times, the disciples had to use their hands to carry out the tasks Jesus assigned. Knowing your Bible is important; don't get me wrong. But being a disciple is more about going and doing. As we mature as Christians, knowledge leads to *action*.

Practical Guide to Making Jesus Famous

When Jesus arrived on our planet, his name was Immanuel, "God with us" (Matthew 1:23). When he left the earth, he promised to be with us to the end of the age (28:20). Jesus is always present, and you can be confident that the Spirit is too. He'll give you everything you need to disciple someone. Having said that, here are some things you can do today to mentor an apprentice of Jesus:

- **Start with family.** Siblings (particularly older ones) can naturally lead their brothers and sisters to walk the path of Jesus. But kids can also lead their parents to Christ—and often do! Your family sees your behavior more than anyone else. So radical loyalty to Jesus and sacrificial love for others can make a huge impact in your home. From your family, you can move outward to circles of friends, teammates, and classmates. Challenge: Make a list of five people you have influence over, and begin to pray daily for them to come to Jesus. Ask God to give you insight and opportunities to share your faith with them.

- **Grab food together.** Meals are spiritual. So invite someone to dinner. You're not trying to corner her for evangelism. You really are just trying to get to know her. As you eat, ask three questions to get to know more about her. These questions may even give you an opportunity to share your own story. Challenge: If you feel comfortable, tell her you typically give God thanks for your meals, and ask whether that would make her uncomfortable. If she says no, you can let her know you pray for her daily and ask, "Is there anything specific you would like me to pray about?"

- **Invite to church.** Most people who come to Christ do so at a local church. So, invite someone to hang out or grab food—but after church this time. Your invite can sound something like this: "There's a group of us going out to eat after church. Would you like to join us?" Remember, however, he doesn't know anything about your church. So an invite to church should also include some details: "Typically the service lasts for an hour, and we wear what we normally wear to school. We can pick you up so we can go together." Most people will say no the first time. That's okay! Statistically, one in three will say yes, but it may take three invites before a person's schedule is open. Challenge: Plan on inviting three people three times. Usually one will say yes.

One final observation. People convert (to anything) when the weight of influence shifts from outside the group to inside. In other words, your friend will convert when the opinions of those inside the church outweigh the opinions of those outside the church. Therefore, evangelism should always be a team sport. The more people your friend knows and respects who follow Christ, the easier it will be for her to make Jesus Lord. When enough of us do this, Jesus's commission will be completed.

Key Points

- We all have insecurity about sharing our faith.
- Don't overcomplicate making disciples. You're simply walking with people in the direction of Jesus.
- Start by inviting someone to a meal and then to church.

This Week

❏ **Day 1 (Eyes):** After reading the essay, answer this question: Are you leading anyone to follow Jesus?

❏ **Day 2 (Ears):** Read Isaiah 19:16–25; 25:1–12. What do these predict about God's desire for Israel?

❏ **Day 3 (Heart):** Think about what Jesus expects us to do now: Romans 10:14–15, 2 Corinthians 5:20, and Colossians 1:28.

❏ **Day 4 (Voice):** Discussion:

- Who was most influential in leading you to Jesus? What did that person do?
- What's keeping you from sharing your faith? How will you overcome those barriers?
- After reading this essay, what would you say is your greatest strength in leading someone to Christ?
- Who are the five people on your daily prayer list that you hope will come to Christ?

❏ **Day 5 (Hands):** Choose one of the three challenges under "Practical Guide to Making Jesus Famous," and do it this week.

51

How Can We Make Jesus Famous?

Biblical Concept: Ascension
Read: Acts 1:9–11

Driving, dating, working—they involve more than we imagined. As kids we look forward to them but soon realize they're bigger than we thought. So it is with the kingdom of God. Jesus broke every expectation of how big the kingdom would be. The disciples *imagined* that Jesus would regather the twelve tribes of the Jews inside the borders of Israel. Instead, he expanded the borders of Israel to include every people group on the planet. The book of Acts describes just how that happened.

What Does Jesus Intend to Accomplish?

After the Resurrection, the disciples asked Jesus, "Lord, will you at this time restore the kingdom to Israel?" (Acts 1:6). They expected Jesus to be the king of their nation. Jesus has his sights set higher. He intends to be the king of all the earth.

The problem was that they underinterpreted the promises, beginning with God's promise to Abraham: "In you *all* the families of the earth shall be blessed" (Genesis 12:3). Isaiah added more clarity: "It shall come to pass in the latter days that the mountain of the house of the LORD shall be established . . . and *all the nations shall flow to it*" (2:2).

The disciples back then undervalued Jesus's spiritual reign over all the earth. Today we tend to undervalue Jesus's earthly reign. Jesus called for a kingdom, not just a church. What's the difference? For starters, a church is led by a preacher; a kingdom is ruled by a king. A church has members; a kingdom has citizens. A church has rules like "don't run in church"; a kingdom has laws, and you can run all you want.

If the church is to fulfill the mission of Jesus, we must think bigger about what we're up to. Our goal isn't just to take people to heaven. Our goal is to bring heaven to earth. Our commission is to extend the reign of Jesus in heaven to every corner of the globe.

How Are We to Expand His Kingdom?

Are you intimidated? You should be. Think of how these fishermen felt. Peter, Andrew, James, and John had no formal training. They were in way over their heads. That's why Acts 1:8 is so important to them—and to us: "You will receive power when the Holy Spirit has come upon you, and you will be my witnesses in Jerusalem and in all Judea and Samaria, and to the end of the earth."

This verse says two things we must not miss. First, the commission won't be accomplished through our efforts alone. It will be accomplished through the power of the Holy Spirit.

Second, Acts 1:8 provides a map of the geographic expansion of the kingdom. It began in Jerusalem (Acts 1–7), then went to Judea and Samaria (Acts 8–12), and ultimately reached the ends of the earth (Acts 13–28). Once again, it was the Spirit who guided the apostles. God does the same for you. He puts you in the right place at the right time for his glory.

The more we are in sync with the Spirit, the more fully we can partner with him. So, what is the Spirit's evangelism strategy? This is obviously an oversimplification, but there are two key elements: (1) *inclusion* of all people and (2) *influence* in every arena—politics, education, religion, entertainment. God moved mountains to take the gospel to *all* nations in Acts. We should too. And we should pay attention to how the Spirit might empower us to use our influence to make Jesus famous.

When Will Jesus Return?

"When he had said these things, as they were looking on, he was lifted up, and a cloud took him out of their sight. And while they were gazing into heaven as he went, behold, two men stood by them in white robes, and said, 'Men of Galilee, why do you stand looking into heaven? This Jesus, who was taken up from you into heaven, will come in the same way as you saw him go into heaven'" (Acts 1:9–11).

This scene describes what has been called the Ascension. Jesus rose to heaven. The two men dressed in white were angels. How do we know? White clothes in the Bible signify God's messengers (Mark 16:5; Luke 24:4; John 20:12). The cloud represents God's presence (Exodus 24:15–18; Luke 9:34–35; 21:27; Revelation 11:12). So, the angels, who had been in God's presence, came to instruct the apostles after Jesus returned to God's presence.

The Ascension hasn't gotten a lot of attention in sermons. However, it's a big deal in the rest of the New Testament (Luke 9:51; John 3:13; Acts 2:32–33; 5:30–31; 7:55; Romans 8:34; Ephesians 1:20–21; 4:8–10; Philippians 2:9–11; Colossians 3:1; 1 Timothy 3:16; Hebrews 1:3; 8:1; 10:12; 1 Peter 3:21–22). So, what is Jesus doing? He is sitting down at the right hand of the Father as our advocate. Paul described the scene in Romans 8:34: "Who is to condemn? Christ Jesus is the one who died—more than that, who was raised—who is at the right hand of God, who indeed is interceding for us." That makes his ascension as important for our salvation as his death and resurrection.

The disciples were so focused on Jesus leaving that they paid no attention to the angels' arrival. That had to be frustrating for the angels. Finally the angels broke the silence: "Men of Galilee, why do you stand looking into heaven?" (Acts 1:11). That was an important question.

When they were with Jesus, they fixated on the past: "Lord, will you at this time restore the kingdom to Israel?" (verse 6). When Jesus left, they focused on the future. But today is the only thing we can control, and we have work to do. There are still entire people groups who haven't been included in the kingdom of Christ. Some are in distant lands, and reaching them will require the strategic effort of the church. Others are already within your circle of influence, and reaching them will require your obedience to the Spirit's promptings. Rather than fixating on the past or focusing on the future, let's get down to the business of preparing people for Jesus's return.

Key Points

- The church of Jesus Christ is a kingdom with citizens, laws, and boundaries.

- The Holy Spirit empowers us to expand the boundaries of Jesus's kingdom to the ends of the earth.

- Jesus will return in the same way he ascended from the earth.

This Week

❏ **Day I (Eyes):** After reading the essay, answer this question: What are you doing to prepare others for Jesus's return?

❏ **Day 2 (Ears):** How is Micah 4:1–8 fulfilled through the church?

❏ **Day 3 (Heart):** Think about the nature of Jesus's current reign: Philippians 2:9–11, Colossians 1:20, and Revelation 19:16.

❏ **Day 4 (Voice):** Discussion:
  • How would you think or act differently if you saw your local church as part of a global kingdom?
  • Describe a time when you felt the Spirit empowering you to share your faith.
  • What circle of influence do you have? It could be with family, with friends, at school, or on a team.
  • What can you do to make Jesus famous within your circle of influence?

❏ **Day 5 (Hands):** Plan a project in your community or at your school, using your influence to make people more aware of Jesus.

52

Who Is Jesus?

Biblical Concept: Return
Read: Revelation 1:13–17; 5:5–6; 19:11–16

Our quest for Jesus ends with Revelation. Many find this book confusing because we keep asking it a question it was never designed to answer: "When is Jesus returning?" If we ask the right questions, however, Revelation is crystal clear. Here's the best question: "Who is Jesus?" Revelation gives us three detailed portraits of Christ. If we fix our eyes on these images of Jesus, we can survive any season of suffering.

Son of Man

"In the midst of the lampstands [was] one like a *son of man*, clothed with a long robe and with a golden sash around his chest. The hairs of his head were white, like white wool, like snow. His eyes were like a flame of fire. . . . When I saw him, I fell at his feet as though dead. But he laid his right hand on me, saying, 'Fear not, I am the first and the last'" (Revelation 1:13–14, 17).

Crazy picture, right? And who is this "son of man"? Son of Man is actually what Jesus called himself. It was a reference to Daniel 7:13–14, where "a son of man" was exalted with "the Ancient of Days," who gave him "dominion and glory and a kingdom, that all peoples, nations, and languages should serve him."

Daniel wondered at the vision. How on earth could a human figure share the glory of the God of heaven? In Revelation we get the answer: Jesus. He is human like us. At the same time, he is all-powerful God. He is our great high priest, and he still says to us, "Fear not."

We may not know when he's returning, but we're certain about what he's doing right now in preparation for his return.

Lamb of God

"One of the elders said to me, 'Weep no more; behold, the Lion of the tribe of Judah, the Root of David, has conquered, so that he can open the scroll and its seven seals.' And between the throne and the four living creatures and among the elders I saw a Lamb standing, as though it had been slain, with seven horns and with seven eyes" (Revelation 5:5–6).

John broke down in tears because no one had the authority to open the scroll. Except one. *The One.* The Lion of the tribe of Judah. The Messiah had conquered, earning him the right to reveal what was in the scroll.

John expected a Lion. Instead, out came a Lamb. He was bloodied and had seven eyes and seven horns. To us he would look like a mutant. But these are biblical codes. Seven represents the work of God among humans. His seven eyes mean he sees all that's going on in the world. Seven horns represent God's complete power to protect us in this world.

More importantly, the Lamb had been slain. He has seen suffering, just like you. What's more? He knows your sin and took the punishment for you. In the Resurrection, the Lamb that was slain rose as a Lion that conquered.

We may not know when he's returning, but we're certain about what he's already done in preparation for his return.

Conquering King

"I saw heaven opened, and behold, a white horse! The one sitting on it is called Faithful and True, and in righteousness he judges and makes war. His eyes are like a flame of fire, and on his head are many diadems, and he has a name written that no one knows but himself. He is clothed in a robe dipped in blood, and the name by which he is called is The Word of God. And the armies of heaven, arrayed in fine linen, white and pure, were following him on white horses. From his mouth comes a sharp sword with which to strike down the nations, and he will rule them with a rod of iron. He will tread the winepress of the fury of the wrath of God the Almighty. On his robe and on his thigh he has a name written, King of kings and Lord of lords" (19:11–16).

When Jesus came to earth the first time, he came as a compassionate shepherd. When he returns, he'll be a conquering king! Just reread that description above. This is raw, unequaled power!

Some have called this the Battle of Armageddon, but there's no battle. Oh sure, the enemy has weapons and a strategy. But according to the Bible, not a single shot is fired. Jesus simply speaks. With a single declaration, he destroys his enemies and establishes his eternal reign.

We may not know when he's returning, but we're certain about what he'll do when we next lay eyes on him in the clouds.

The Purpose of the Portraits

Each of these three portraits comes right before a problem Christians face. Right after chapter 1, Jesus sends seven letters to the seven churches. They were struggling with the same things we struggle with today. But every problem the church faces can be solved by a clear view of Jesus, the Son of Man. Keep your eyes on him.

Chapter 5 is followed by the tribulation described in Revelation 6–18. The world is full of evil, disasters, and pain. But there is hope. Jesus, the Lamb that was slain, is also the Lion that conquers. Every struggle you have with sin and suffering is conquerable through the blood of the Lamb and the power of the Lion. Keep your eyes on him.

Chapter 19 comes right before the final judgment. No doubt, we face uncertain days and dangerous battles. Nonetheless, Jesus, with a mere word, will overcome our enemies and bring us safely into eternity (verses 17–21). In the darkest night of the soul, one glimpse of the conquering King, whose coming is sure, will relieve our weary hearts. Keep your eyes on him.

He is the ultimate end of our quest.

Key Points

- Looking to Jesus, the Son of Man, solves every problem the church faces.

- Looking to Jesus, the slain Lamb, comforts us in all the pain we experience.

- Looking to Jesus, the conquering King, overcomes all our worries about an uncertain future.

This Week

☐ **Day 1 (Eyes):** After reading the essay, answer this question: How do you see Jesus?

☐ **Day 2 (Ears):** Read Daniel 7:9–14. What did Jesus look like before coming to earth?

☐ **Day 3 (Heart):** Think about how you should respond to Jesus: Revelation 1:17; 5:12–13; and 19:6–8.

☐ **Day 4 (Voice):** Discussion:

- Do you have a picture of Jesus in your home? What does it look like?
- As you reflect on this past year's quest, what has surprised you about Jesus?
- Which concerns you most right now: (1) the state of your church, (2) the trials you face, or (3) the uncertainty of the future? Which portrait of Jesus speaks to that?
- If Jesus returned right now, what would you wish you had done in the last month to prepare for his coming?

☐ **Day 5 (Hands):** What do you need to do to continue your quest, chasing after the heart of Jesus? Identify your next steps.

Overview

#	Section/Series	Question	Concept	Day 2	Day 3
	Person: Beginning				
1	John 1:1–18	Is God Jesus?	Incarnation	Pss. 2; 110	Rom. 9:5; Titus 2:13; Heb. 1:8
2	Matt. 1:1–17	Is life random?	Genealogy	Josh. 2; 6	Gal. 4:4; Heb. 11:31; James 2:25
3	Luke 1:26–45	Can God use me for big things?	Annunciation	Isa. 9:1–7	Col. 1:15–17; Heb. 1:3; Rev. 1:8
4	Luke 2:1–20	Does God play favorites?	Nativity	Ps. 23; John 10:1–18	Matt. 23:12; James 4:10; 1 Pet. 5:5–6
	Person: Purpose				
5	Luke 2:41–52	Did Jesus know he was God when he was a boy?	Jesus's maturity	1 Sam. 24	Rom. 13:3–7; Eph. 6:2–3; 1 Tim. 5:17
6	Mark 1:1–13	If Jesus was perfect, why was he baptized?	Baptism	Num. 13–14	Rom. 6:1–7; 1 Cor. 10:1–5

#	Section/ Series	Question	Concept	Day 2	Day 3
7	Luke 19:1–10	Did Jesus have a life purpose?	Life purpose	Eccles. 5:8–6:12	Rom. 1:16; 2 Tim. 1:7–8; 1 Pet. 3:15–16
8	Mark 10:32–45	Did Jesus have a life purpose?	Life purpose	Josh. 1	1 Cor. 9:19; 2 Cor. 4:5; 1 Pet. 5:2–3
	Person: Relationships				
9	Luke 5:1–11	How do I recognize God's call on my life?	Calling	1 Sam. 3	2 Cor. 5:20; 1 Pet. 2:9–10; 4:10–11
10	Mark 3:31–35	How do you get into Jesus's inner circle?	Family	Isa. 49	1 Cor. 12:13; Eph. 2:14; Col. 3:11
11	Luke 7:36–50	Does my past determine my future?	Shame	Exod. 2:11–4:17	Rom. 8:1; 1 Tim. 1:15; 1 John 1:9
12	John 3:1–21	Who are social influencers for Jesus?	Influence	1 Sam. 10:9–27; 13:1–15	Acts 10:34; Rom. 2:11; James 2:1–7
13	John 4:4–42	Who are social influencers for Jesus?	Influence	2 Kings 6:24–7:20	Rom. 1:16; 1 Cor. 1:20; 3:18–19
	Power: Wonders				
14	John 2:1–12	Is Christianity boring?	Celebration	Song of Sol. 5	2 Cor. 11:2; Eph. 5:23; Rev. 21:9
15	Mark 4:35–5:20	Can Jesus turn my storm into a story?	Chaos	Ps. 2	Eph. 1:20–21; Col. 2:9; Rev. 1:17–18
16	Mark 6:31–52	Can Jesus provide for my needs?	Provision	Exod. 16	Acts 20:28; 1 Pet. 2:25; Rev. 7:17

#	Section/ Series	Question	Concept	Day 2	Day 3
17	Mark 9:2–13	Is Jesus really divine?	Divinity	Mal. 3–4	2 Cor. 3:7; Phil. 2:8–11; 2 Pet. 1:16–18
	Power: Signs				
18	Mark 1:29–39	Does Jesus care about my pain?	Pain	Lev. 26:1–26	Heb. 12:12–13; James 5:16; 1 Pet. 2:24
19	Mark 1:40–45	Can Jesus make me clean?	Purity	2 Kings 5	2 Cor. 7:1; Eph. 5:26; 2 Tim. 2:21
20	Luke 7:1–10	Is Jesus impressed with me?	Inclusion	Gen. 12:1–9; 14:1–24	Acts 10:1–8, 22–23, 28–29, 34–35
21	Mark 5:21–43	Can Jesus restore my relationships?	Restoration	Ruth	Luke 8:2–3; Phil. 4:2–3; James 2:25
22	John 11:17–44	Can Jesus give me life?	Life	1 Kings 17:8–24; 2 Kings 4:18–37	1 Cor. 6:14; 15:20–28; 2 Cor. 4:14
	Power: Claims				
23	Mark 2:1–17	Can Jesus forgive me?	Forgiveness	Ps. 32	Rom. 4:7; Eph. 1:7; Heb. 9:22
24	John 5:1–18	What do we need from Jesus?	Loyalty	1 Sam. 18:1–4; 19:1–7; 20:1–42	Rom. 4:5; Col. 1:23; 1 Thess. 1:3
25	John 9:1–41	Can Jesus help me see clearly?	Clarity	2 Sam. 22	2 Cor. 4:6; Eph. 1:18; Rev. 3:17
26	Matt. 12:22–45	Can Jesus accept me?	Liberation	Jonah	Heb. 6:4–6; 10:26; 1 John 5:16

#	Section/ Series	Question	Concept	Day 2	Day 3
	Preaching: Teaching				
27	Luke 4:16–30	What did Jesus say about social justice?	Justice	1 Kings 17:8–24; 2 Kings 5:1–14	Acts 13:46; Rom. 1:16; 2:9–10
28	Matt. 5:3–20	What did Jesus say about morality?	Ethics	Exod. 20:1–17	Rom. 13:9; Gal. 5:13; 1 John 3:16–18
29	Matt. 6:1–18	What did Jesus say about religious duties?	Piety	1 Sam. 13; 17	Gal. 1:10; Col. 3:23; 1 Thess. 2:4
30	Matt. 6:19–34	Why does Jesus care so much about my money?	Wealth	Prov. (selections)	Eph. 5:5; 1 Tim. 6:17–19; Heb. 13:5
	Preaching: Stories				
31	Luke 15:11–32	How does Jesus feel about prodigals?	Prodigals	2 Chron. 7:11–22	Acts 3:19; 2 Cor. 7:9–10; 1 Pet. 2:25
32	Matt. 13:1–23	How do I hear God's voice?	Parables	Isa. 6	Acts 28:26–27; Rom. 11:8; 2 Cor. 3:14
33	Luke 10:25–37	How can I be sure I'm saved?	Bias	Lev. 19:9–18; Deut. 6	1 John 3:15–16; 4:16–21; 5:13
34	John 10:1–21	How did Jesus lead?	Leadership	Ezek. 34	Heb. 13:20; 1 Pet. 2:25; 5:4
	Preaching: Training				
35	Matt. 10:1–42	How can we share our faith effectively?	Evangelism	Exod. 3–4	Rom. 10:9–10; Heb. 13:15; 1 Pet. 3:15

#	Section/ Series	Question	Concept	Day 2	Day 3
36	Matt. 11:2–11	Do you ever doubt your doubts?	Resilience	Isa. 42:1–4; 49:1–6; 50:4–9; 52:13–53:12	Rom. 8:14–17; 2 Cor. 3:17–18; Eph. 1:13
37	Mark 7:1–23	What makes you a good person?	Morality	Isa. 58	Acts 15:20; Rom. 14:14; 1 Cor. 8:7
38	Matt. 16:13–28	Who do you say Jesus is?	Declaration	1 Kings 12	2 Cor. 4:10–12; Gal. 2:20; Phil. 3:10–11
39	Luke 10:38–42	What's worth worrying about?	Anxiety	Ps. 37	Phil. 4:6
	Passion: Preparation				
40	Luke 19:29–44	Was Jesus political?	Politics	Ps. 118	Acts 17:7; 1 Cor. 15:24–25; Rev. 11:15
41	Mark 11:12–25	Was Jesus political?	Authority	Isa. 56:1–8; Jer. 7:1–11	1 Cor. 6:16–19; 2 Cor. 6:16; Eph. 2:19–22
42	John 13:1–20	Was Jesus full of himself?	Humility	Dan. 4	Rom. 7:6; 2 Cor. 4:5; Gal. 5:13
43	Mark 14:1–25	What did Jesus think about himself?	Sacrament	Exod. 12	1 Cor. 5:7; 1 Pet. 1:19; Rev. 5:12
	Passion: Suffering				
44	John 14:1–31	How can I survive difficult days?	Hope	Ezek. 36:22–36; Joel 2:28–32	John 1:18; Acts 4:12; Heb. 1:3
45	Mark 14:32–52	How can we learn grit from how Jesus suffered?	Suffering	2 Sam. 15	Rom. 8:17; Col. 1:24; 1 Pet. 2:21–23

#	Section/ Series	Question	Concept	Day 2	Day 3
46	Mark 14:53–72	How do you stay in control in a crisis?	Opposition	Ps. 88	2 Cor. 4:16–18; Heb. 2:18; James 1:2–4
47	Matt. 27:11–26	How do you endure pain?	Endurance	Isa. 52:13–53:12	Rom. 5:10; 12:20; Heb. 10:12–13
48	Matt. 27:27–50	Why did Jesus die?	Atonement	Ps. 22	Rom. 3:21–26; 2 Cor. 5:21; Heb. 9:26–28
	Passion: Victory				
49	John 20	Did Jesus really rise from the dead?	Resurrection	Ps. 16	1 Cor. 15:3–8; 1 Thess. 4:14; 1 John 1:1–2
50	Matt. 28:16–20	What does Jesus expect us to do now?	Commission	Isa. 19:16–25; 25:1–12	Rom. 10:14–15; 2 Cor. 5:20; Col. 1:28
51	Acts 1:9–11	How can we make Jesus famous?	Ascension	Mic. 4:1–8	Phil. 2:9–11; Col. 1:20; Rev. 19:16
52	Rev. 1:13–17; 5:5–6; 19:11–16	Who is Jesus?	Return	Dan. 7:9–14	Rev. 1:17; 5:12–13; 19:6–8

Notes

Chapter 2: Is Life Random?

1. For those of you who actually did fact-check me, congratulations, you get a digital gold star. Just for clarity, we count Jeconiah in the third section, after the Exile, since that is where Matthew puts him in verse 12.

Chapter 12: Who Are Social Influencers for Jesus? Part 1

1. William Barclay, *The New Daily Study Bible, The Letter to the Hebrews* (Louisville, KY: Westminster John Knox, 2002), 145.

Chapter 19: Can Jesus Make Me Clean?

1. From an ancient midrash on Leviticus, Leviticus Rabbah. Vayikra Rabbah 16:3, Sefaria, www.sefaria.org/Vayikra_Rabbah.16?lang=en.

Chapter 23: Can Jesus Forgive Me?

1. Alfred Edersheim, *The Life and Times of Jesus the Messiah,* 8th ed. (New York: Longmans, Green, 1899), 1:516.

Chapter 30: Why Does Jesus Care So Much About My Money?

1. Bob Dylan, "Gotta Serve Somebody," *Slow Train Coming,* Sony Music Entertainment, 1979.
2. "Facts & Statistics," Anxiety & Depression Association of America, https://adaa.org/about-adaa/press-room/facts-statistics.
3. Alison Escalante, MD, "U.S. Leads in the Worldwide Anxiety Epidemic," *Psychology Today,* April 26, 2019, www.psychologytoday.com/us/blog/shouldstorm/201904/us-leads-in-the-worldwide-anxiety-epidemic.

4. Alexander Konnopka and Hannah Konig, "Economic Burden of Anxiety Disorders: A Systematic Review and Meta-Analysis," *Pharmaco-
   economics,* January 2020, https://pubmed.ncbi.nlm.nih.gov/31646432.

Chapter 39: What's Worth Worrying About?

1. Sharon Begley, "In the Age of Anxiety, Are We All Mentally Ill?,"
   Reuters, July 13, 2012, www.reuters.com/article/us-usa-health-anxiety
   /in-the-age-of-anxiety-are-we-all-mentally-ill-idUSBRE86C07820120713.
2. "Facts & Statistics," Anxiety & Depression Association of America,
   https://adaa.org/about-adaa/press-room/facts-statistics.
3. You can also view this video at Mark Moore, "Core 52, Lesson 48:
   Worry (Philippians 4:6)," August 31, 2019, YouTube video, 6:20, www
   .youtube.com/watch?v=5RBPGuryFkQ.

Mark E. Moore, bestselling author of *Core 52,* is a teaching pastor at Christ's Church of the Valley in Phoenix, Arizona, one of the fastest-growing and most dynamic churches in America. He previously spent two decades as a New Testament professor at Ozark Christian College. His goal is to make Scripture accessible and relevant to people trying to make sense of Christianity. Mark and his wife, Barbara, live in Phoenix.

About the Type

This book was set in Garamond, a typeface originally designed by the Parisian type cutter Claude Garamond (c. 1500–61). This version of Garamond was modeled on a 1592 specimen sheet from the Egenolff-Berner foundry, which was produced from types assumed to have been brought to Frankfurt by the punch cutter Jacques Sabon (c. 1520–80).

Claude Garamond's distinguished romans and italics first appeared in *Opera Ciceronis* in 1543–44. The Garamond types are clear, open, and elegant.

Did *Quest 52 Student Edition* move you?
Challenge you?
Motivate you?

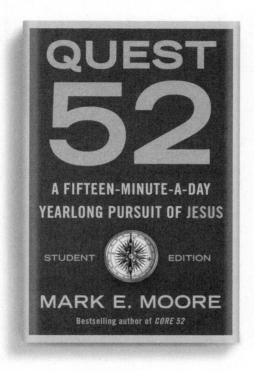

Share your thoughts with Pastor Mark about how *Quest 52 Student Edition* inspired you at **Quest52.org/Quest52Stories**

Check out *Quest 52*! Read with your parents, grandparents, or other adults.